Practice Perfect Softball

National Fastpitch Coaches Association

NATIONAL FASTPITCH
COACHES ASSOCIATION

JoAnne Graf, PhD
Editor

Library of Congress Cataloging-in-Publication Data

Names: National Fastpitch Coaches Association.
Title: Practice perfect softball / National Fastpitch Coaches Association.
Description: Champaign, IL : Human Kinetics, [2016] | Includes
 bibliographical references.
Identifiers: LCCN 2015049141 | ISBN 9781492513544 (print)
Subjects: LCSH: Softball--Training. | Pitching (Softball) |
 Softball--Coaching.
Classification: LCC GV881.4.T72 P73 2016 | DDC 796.357/8--dc23 LC record available at http://lccn.loc.gov/2015049141

ISBN: 978-1-4925-1354-4 (print)

The web addresses cited in this text were current as of March 2016, unless otherwise noted.

Acquisitions Editor: Justin Klug; **Developmental Editor:** Anne Hall; **Managing Editor**: Nicole O'Dell; **Copyeditor:** Bob Replinger; **Permissions Manager:** Martha Gullo; **Graphic Designer:** Denise Lowry; **Cover Designer:** Keith Blomberg; **Photograph (cover):** © Human Kinetics; **Photo Production Manager:** Jason Allen; **Art Manager:** Kelly Hendren; **Associate Art Manager:** Alan L. Wilborn; **Illustrations:** © Human Kinetics; **Printer:** United Graphics

Human Kinetics books are available at special discounts for bulk purchase. Special editions or book excerpts can also be created to specification. For details, contact the Special Sales Manager at Human Kinetics.

Printed in the United States of America   10   9   8   7   6   5   4   3   2   1

The paper in this book is certified under a sustainable forestry program.

Human Kinetics
Website: www.HumanKinetics.com

United States: Human Kinetics, P.O. Box 5076, Champaign, IL 61825-5076
800-747-4457
e-mail: info@hkusa.com

Canada: Human Kinetics, 475 Devonshire Road Unit 100, Windsor, ON N8Y 2L5
800-465-7301 (in Canada only)
e-mail: info@hkcanada.com

Europe: Human Kinetics, 107 Bradford Road, Stanningley, Leeds LS28 6AT, United Kingdom
+44 (0) 113 255 5665
e-mail: hk@hkeurope.com

Australia: Human Kinetics, 57A Price Avenue, Lower Mitcham, South Australia 5062
08 8372 0999
e-mail: info@hkaustralia.com

New Zealand: Human Kinetics, P.O. Box 80, Mitcham Shopping Centre, South Australia 5062
0800 222 062
e-mail: info@hknewzealand.com

E6617

Practice Perfect Softball

Contents

Preface   vi

Key to Diagrams   viii

Chapter 1   **Establishing a Strong Work Ethic**   **1**
             Julie Lenhart

Chapter 2   **Planning Productive Practices**   **7**
             Rachel Hanson

Chapter 3   **Incorporating Technology and Practice Tools**   **21**
             Beverly Smith

Chapter 4   **Identifying Strengths and Weaknesses**   **33**
             Rachel Lawson

Chapter 5   **Developing a Competitive Environment**   **45**
             Lisa (Sweeney) Van Ackeren

Chapter 6   **Motivating Players in Practices**   **57**
             Dot Richardson, MD

Chapter 7   **Organizing Effective Batting Practices**   **67**
             Ken Eriksen

Chapter 8	**Organizing Effective Fielding Practices**	**75**
	Celeste Knierim	
Chapter 9	**Developing the Pitcher and Catcher**	**97**
	Connie Clark	
Chapter 10	**Perfecting Position Play**	**113**
	Bill Gray and Melissa Chmielewski	
Chapter 11	**Offensive Situational Practices**	**135**
	Lonni Alameda	
Chapter 12	**Defensive Situational Practices**	**147**
	Jo Evans	
Chapter 13	**Evaluating Practices**	**157**
	Donna Papa	
Chapter 14	**Practicing Indoors**	**167**
	Jen McIntyre	
Appendix	**Sample Practice Plans**	**181**

About the NFCA   208

About the Editor   208

About the Contributors   209

Preface

When I was approached about editing a book about softball practices, I eagerly said I would love to be involved in the project. The reason is simple: Coaching is a passion that has consumed my career. A good coach is not only a coach but also an academic advisor, motivator, role model, marketer, strength coach, nutritionist, sports psychologist, and more. Most important, a great coach helps players improve to reach their highest potential, which happens through practice. Creating exciting and innovative practices is a challenge for every coach. This book will help you improve your practices to maximize the potential of your team.

We have all heard the quotation by Vince Lombardi: "Practice does not make perfect. Perfect practice makes perfect." *Practice Perfect Softball* is made up of chapters written by the most knowledgeable softball coaches in the country. The authors have reached the highest level in their profession including the National Fastpitch Softball Coaches Hall of Fame, USA national team coach, Olympic gold medalist, conference coaches of the year, NCAA College World Series coaches, and so on. These coaches have given their valuable time to pass along their secrets to improving softball practices so that your players will be excited about going to practice. They will be motivated to work hard, which will help them improve. As players work hard, improvement follows and wins come more frequently. The chapters will give you insights into practice organization, hitting drills, motivational tips, specific positional drills, practice evaluation, inside drills, using technology in your practices, and developing competitive practices.

I cannot thank these coaches enough for giving their time. As a former coach, I know how valuable their time is. Giving back to the softball coaching profession is what makes the NFCA coaches special. They love sharing their knowledge, which you can use to improve your team. You can incorporate the information included in this book into your practices.

Lacy Lee Baker, the former executive director of the National Fastpitch Coaches Association (NFCA), deserves a great deal of credit for incorporating education into the goals of the NFCA. She pioneered many forms of coaching education including *The Softball Coaching Bible I* and *II*, *Practice Perfect Softball*, NFCA coaches' college courses, convention clinic sessions, *Fastpitch Delivery*, satellite umpire clinics, and the NFCA website. When you see an NFCA coach, don't hesitate to ask the questions that you want answered to help you improve as a coach. They will be happy to help. When I asked these coaches to write a chapter for this book, they eagerly said yes. *Practice Perfect Softball* will help you to make your practices perfect.

In conclusion, thank you to all the coaches and players who make the game of softball great.

Key to Diagrams

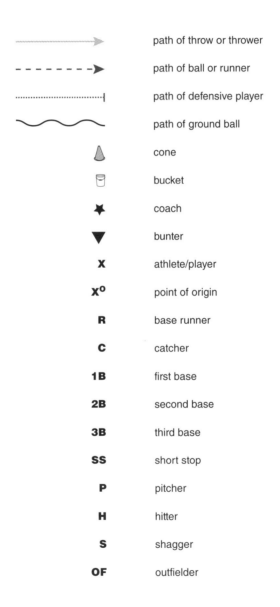

⟶	path of throw or thrower
⇢	path of ball or runner
·············⊣	path of defensive player
∿	path of ground ball
△	cone
⊟	bucket
✦	coach
▼	bunter
X	athlete/player
X°	point of origin
R	base runner
C	catcher
1B	first base
2B	second base
3B	third base
SS	short stop
P	pitcher
H	hitter
S	shagger
OF	outfielder

Chapter 1

Establishing a Strong Work Ethic

Julie Lenhart

To establish a strong work ethic, we as coaches must create a learning environment in practice that doesn't reflect the tedious and often dreaded grind associated with work. The best part of the day is practice—that's why it's called playing the game, not working the game. Sometimes we become so wrapped up in attempting to achieve perfection that we miss the fun of game. The hours we spend lifting weights, doing mental training, taking in proper nutrition, studying, and finally actually practicing become entrenched in a more-is-more mentality. Kicking back at times and focusing on what makes softball an enjoyable sport allows us to see that many times the less-is-more philosophy works, too. The trick to establishing a strong work ethic in practice is allowing it to feel like play, not work.

Obviously, to compete and win at a high level, the intensity at practice must match or exceed the intensity of the actual game. A team can't practice at one level and expect to compete at a different level. Practices must cultivate motivated learning. Anson Dorrance, the extremely successful women's soccer coach at the University of North Carolina, Chapel Hill, describes it as transcending ordinary effort:

> Ordinary effort is when you're comfortable. That's mediocrity. A lot of athletes work within their comfort zone, physically and technically. They don't feel like they're going to lose control, or pass out from fatigue. But when you train within your comfort zone, you're not preparing yourself for a match. In a game situation, the other team is trying to take you out of your comfort zone. So, as soon as they

do, you're in unfamiliar territory. You panic. You make a mistake, or lose the ball. The challenge for you as an individual athlete is to find a way to elevate your environment. This is not easy. You likely have to set your own standards of practice performance. You are part of a team sport, in which coaches and your teammates are critical for motivation. It's tough to keep yourself on this edge independently. But this is what sets the truly great players apart. It is their capacity to do what I call "flame on"—to hit a button and just ignite. They can do this whenever, and with whomever.

> Excerpted from *The Vision of a Champion—Advice and Inspiration form the World's Most Successful Women's Soccer Coach*, by Anson Dorrance and Gloria Averbuch, 2005, Huron River Press.

Competition in Practice

We associate pressure with opportunity. In other words, instead of calling it a pressure situation, call it an opportunity situation. In practice, we provide drills in which people compete against each other, which automatically amps up the intensity and work ethic. Here are a few examples.

Minute to Win It

Use your imagination to create groups to compete against each other. Corners versus middles would be one option. Corners have one minute to see how many perfect throws to the plate they can execute from ground balls that the coach hits alternately to third and first. Middles get their minute to see whether they can beat the corners' total. You could use right side versus left side, pit defense A against defense B, add outfielders to the groups, or use any other combination you can think of.

Get 'Em On, Get 'Em Over, Get 'Em Home

Each batter competes against the pitcher (or machine). The hitter gets three at-bats. She attempts to get on (base hit), bunt to move the runner, and then drive a base hit to score the run. Each at-bat is worth one point. See who wins—pitcher or hitter.

7 Up

The number 7 is used to represent seven innings. Each fielder must execute seven perfect plays in a row (ground ball or fly ball with a good throw to first base). An error on the number of balls hit to the fielder results in the same number of sprints. For example, an error on the first ball hit requires one sprint, and an error on the seventh ball hit means seven sprints. The first inning is the same as the seventh inning, although the pressure to perform builds. This drill requires players to perform no matter which inning it is.

Pitcher Progression Challenge

I learned this drill from Megan Walker, the pitching coach at Ithaca College. The pitcher must hit the location that the catcher gives her for the pitch before she can move on to the next progression. The first pitcher to finish the progression wins. For example, the pitcher has a fastball, changeup, screw, curve, and drop. She must hit the fastball location given by the catcher before she can move on to the changeup, and so on down the line. When she has hit one of every pitch she throws, she moves on to the next round (hitting two of every pitch, three of every pitch, and so on, figures 1.1 and 1.2). Depending on the time allotted for the workout and the pitch count desired, the rounds and number of pitch types thrown can be adjusted.

Any time you can add competition to the drills in practice, you will notice an increase in intensity. Keeping score with point values (who scores more) or time elements (how many can be completed in a certain time) is all you need to do.

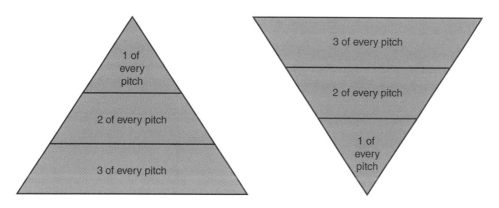

Figure 1.1   Pitching pyramid.   **Figure 1.2**   Inverted pitching pyramid.

Ubuntu

Every year at Cortland we begin the season with a word or phrase describing the focus for that particular team. A few years ago my assistant coach, Brad Posner, told me about a *Sports Illustrated* article ("So Far . . . So Great," Jack McCallum, *Sports Illustrated*, January 14, 2008, vol. 108, issue 1) describing the Boston Celtics and the focus word that helped guide them to a championship. Originating from South Africa, this word was *ubuntu*. The word is tough to define and translate into the English language, but it basically means collective success. For an individual to reach her highest potential, everyone else on the team must do her part to become the best, too. The collective effort of all elevates the team to reach the highest level. The solitary individual doesn't exist. You need to be all you can be because that is the only way I can be all I can be. This statement is a powerful and descriptive way to define work ethic.

We have adopted that word and chant, "I am; we are" before every game during our pregame huddle. This custom is our way of emphasizing the *ubuntu* philosophy. The "I am; we are" mentality promotes an emphasis on team success rather than individual success. When each person strives to be the best, the result will be team success. I think that this is the driving force toward establishing a strong work ethic. The push comes from the upperclassmen down—enforcement from within the team—and the feeling of worth from inside each person.

Athletes don't have to like their role; they just need to accept it and realize how it fits into the *ubuntu* philosophy. Strength is depth, and the ultimate goal of a successful team is having all players practice with the same effort and intensity no matter how many innings they play. Players should adopt the-next-one-up mentality. They should always practice as if they are the next one up, as if they are a starter.

What's Your Why?

Practices must cultivate motivated learning. A strong work ethic is created by motivating athletes to continue to improve and in instilling the drive never to be satisfied at their current level. Athletes are motivated in many ways, and finding what works best for your team is the foundation of creating a strong work ethic in your program. One student introduced me to Eric Thomas, an energetic motivational speaker. This student was preparing a class presentation on motivation and shared with me a video produced by Thomas. The video uses the phrase "What's your why?" to describe what it takes to encourage athletes to strive for perfection. Thomas has produced several online videos that demonstrate the passion he has for this mantra. These videos can inspire your team.

Here is a suggested activity for your team. At the beginning of the season have your team watch Eric Thomas's "What's Your Why?" video and have each team member take a moment to write down and explain her "why" on a notecard. The athlete and the coach need to identify what is important to them. Distinguishing what drives them to perform signifies a purpose to accomplish high standards. Keeping the passion and love of the game alive contributes to a higher level of commitment to intensity in practice. The coach can't be the initiator and cheerleader for enthusiasm and energy. It must come from the athlete. Remind your athletes that they control only two things—attitude and effort. Identifying and reinforcing the drive of why they play softball will help produce a positive attitude and extraordinary effort. Practices will be fun and intense.

Motivating Athletes to Adopt a Strong Work Ethic

You will notice that athletes are motivated by intrinsic (internal) and extrinsic (external) incentives. Intrinsic motivation comes from the pleasure and sense of satisfaction that a person gains from accomplishing a task or skill. It is a sense of accomplishment. The player has a feeling of worth and importance on the team. I think that this is the most important ingredient of a strong work ethic. Here are a few examples of how we use intrinsic motivation in our program.

One of the most important days of our season is the opening meeting before our first practice. Each athlete is given a sheet of paper titled "Hold the Rope." I'm not certain where this analogy originated, but I was introduced to it early in my coaching career. The basic message of the story is that the team that wins the championship every year is not always the most talented team, but the team that "held the rope." Imagine you are hanging off a cliff and the only thing saving you is a rope with the teammate of your choice on the other end. When you can say that everyone on the team would hold the rope for you and that you would hold the rope for every member of the team, that is the definition of holding the rope. It doesn't happen overnight, but the intrinsic feeling of worth and value is extremely powerful. It is the driving force in practice and produces hard work.

Another example of intrinsic motivation happens when we pass out uniforms. When an athlete receives her jersey, she has jumped the final hurdle and has officially joined the softball program. Athletes take great pride in their jersey numbers. Don't you still remember your number? Most athletes attach their number to their signature when they sign their name. We know that the tradition of the past teams has built the foundation for our program. After they graduate, past players always want to know who has their number. A list containing all the names of players who have worn that jersey number is hung in the locker for the current team member to see every day. Players realize and appreciate the fact that their name is now included on that list. The intrinsic drive to represent that number has begun. When alumni come back to campus, we always introduce them to the athlete wearing their old number. Team members need to be aware of the tradition and history of their number and the alumni it represents. This tradition can be an important driving force in your program.

The last example of intrinsic motivation involves hitting hands. Whether it is a high five or a unique handshake, we attempt to hit hands throughout practice. When we rotate in the weight room, athletes hit hands. After drills before a water break, we run through and hit hands. During our dynamic warm-up, we hit hands. The concept of one team, one family is reinforced daily. This feeling of worth and respect is accomplished with a simple hit of the hand. No one is excluded, and the feeling of team is strengthened.

Extrinsic motivation comes from performances that earn rewards and other tangible objects (trophies, all-conference selection, captain). It can also be associated with the incentive to avoid punishment (doing sprints or being screamed at). Extrinsic motivation can take the form of earning helmet stickers or simply being excused from putting equipment away after practice. Another popular incentive is being able to go to the front of the line at dinner. The pursuit of a championship ring or an all-conference trophy can be the driving force behind hard work. The personal achievement of being chosen as team captain can fit both categories of incentive. Using these tactics to find the player's "why" is instrumental in maintaining a strong work ethic.

Barking Dog Philosophy

Fear tactics don't work for me. I don't equate a strong work ethic with using fear associated with being yelled at or being forced to complete a physical punishment. I'm not certain where I heard this analogy of the barking dog, but the concept perfectly describes my coaching style.

Imagine walking on a sidewalk. When you pass a particular house, the curtains open up and a ferocious dog jumps at the window, barking wildly at you. You instantly jump back. The situation has gained your full attention and focus. The next time you walk by that same house, you remember the dog and expect the barking. Your attention is heightened, but the level of anxiety is lower because you expected to see and hear the dog. After the next couple of times of passing the house, you hardly notice the dog anymore and tune it out as you go on your way. The same thing happens when a coach yells at a team (or a parent yells at a child). The first time garners full attention and a focus on every word. When the ranting becomes an everyday experience, it is soon tuned out and the anticipated outcome is not be reached. Many times, the words are not even heard.

No one likes to be barked at. I don't think that a strong work ethic has a direct correlation to a high level of screaming and punishment. When a coach yells infrequently, however, the point is emphasized and players understand it better. The message grabs their attention, and the intensity level is positively affected.

The ultimate goal is to motivate athletes to adopt a strong work ethic. What works for some will not work for others. Your job as a coach is to figure out what formula works best for your team every year. When your athletes accept and buy in to the mentality of we over me and push each other to become the best they can be—no matter what their role is—you've created the work ethic it takes to become a champion! Doing this without making it feel like work is the trick. Remember that practice is the best part of the day.

Chapter 2

Planning Productive Practices

Rachel Hanson

A close look at many great coaches across various sports shows a convincing pattern. In each case, excellence does not happen by accident. Instead, it is developed by focusing on the daily habits that encompass excellence. Before diving into the details of practice planning, we need to establish the philosophical basis for how to practice and play. Several important concepts to emphasize are attention to detail, competitive nature, time management, and organization and structure.

Attention to Detail

A great way to incorporate attention to detail at the start of every practice is to have a set of recurring basic skill repetitions, which will be covered in depth in the section on defense. As you introduce higher-level skills (live game-play scenarios, as an example) be sure to stay focused on high-level execution of the basic skills. Finally, you should balance this approach with a *growth mind-set*, a term coined by Stanford psychology professor Carol Dweck. With a growth mind-set, players are encouraged to practice at the end range of their abilities, which will necessarily lead to mistakes and failure. Those failures are a necessary component of growth, and they must be balanced with feedback on mistakes. This balance allows players to tackle challenges head on, regardless of the potential for failure.

Competitive Nature

The second concept, competitive nature, brings out the best in players as they push each other and themselves to beat out someone else and be their best self. An up-tempo pace, is an important aspect because the game should be easier than practice; ideally, players should be pushed to the edge of their ability level on a daily basis. Finally, the efficient approach is important in helping players get in the maximum number of repetitions while leaving them plenty of time to be students and people outside the sport they play. We'll detail each of those areas later in the chapter, but in many ways the concepts and aspects of the game that you value set the template for what type of practice you want to run. A useful exercise is to spend some time defining the aspects of organizing a practice and running a program that are most important to you and then making sure that those qualities are reflected in your practice plans. For head coaches, I encourage you to do this exercise by yourself before walking through it with your staff. You should be able to present a clear vision for how you want to run practices based on the core values that you believe to be most valuable.

When planning practice, start by taking a step back for a big-picture view; begin with the end in mind. Endless variations of practice could be constructed, and it would be easy to forget certain aspects of the game or neglect to practice some of the core skills. Before starting any practice segment (fall, preseason, in season) our staff looks at the positional skills overview sheets (see table 2.1). We then map out a rough weekly or monthly schedule of what we want to accomplish. Establishing this overview gives us a guideline to work from and ensures that we hit all facets of the game before opening weekend. After you have a template in place, planning the details of any given practice on a daily basis is much easier. As you progress through a typical session, you'll want to increase complexity, intensity, and pace gradually over the course of a full practice.

Time Management

An efficient and well-executed practice shouldn't go beyond two to two and a half hours. Live scrimmages can go as long as three hours. We typically have 10-minute rotations in practice until we get to live aspects. Practically, this schedule plays out as follows: We practice a specific set of skills for approximately 10 minutes, move into one to two small-group skills sessions, move into a live defensive portion, and finally transition to offense. This approach keeps players focused and engaged over the course of a practice. If you find that your practice consistently stretches beyond the two-and-half-hour mark, take a close look to determine whether you're truly being efficient. You may find that the drills are poorly constructed or the pace of practice is too slow in general.

Organization and Structure

Although the details of our practice vary, the overall structure stays consistent, so our players have a general idea of our routine and can move quickly and efficiently through the practice. A typical practice for us includes a short introduction; a full-body warm-up that includes an arm care routine and catch, throw, receive; a defense segment that includes daily skill repetition (the fundamentals), small skills groups, bigger skills groups, and a live element; pitching; and an offensive segment. End with a challenge or a game.

Let's dive into the specifics of each of those sections.

Introduction

We usually start with a 5- to 10-minute practice introduction that begins to get our players into practice mode. We use this time in a variety of ways—to check in with the team physically or mentally, to talk about a value we're working on as a team, or to talk through what we want to accomplish in practice that day. As the coach, you have this time to set the tone for practice. On occasion, you may recognize that the players are physically or mentally drained (midterms or finals weeks for us) and might need a lighthearted start to practice followed by a reminder to leave the day at the gate and focus on practice for the next couple of hours. Make sure that you as the coach set aside the frustrations or pressures of the day and give the team your all with a positive attitude and productive mind-set. If you bring in your personal pressures, you can be sure that the team will pick up on it. A less-than-productive practice will likely ensue. If we want players to learn the self-discipline to attack the practice even after a rough day, it has to start with us.

Warm-Up

This part of practice must be intentionally designed because it can be the difference between healthy bodies and pulled muscles. Depending on time of year, this portion can last 10 to 20 minutes. In fall when their bodies are fresh, we may need only 10 minutes. In the middle of the season when their bodies are worn down and tight, we may need up to 20 minutes. Help your players understand the different levels of fatigue, pain, and injury and make sure they have a voice to let you know what their bodies might need on any particular day.

Table 2.1 Positional Skills List

Offensive			
Hitting	**Bunting**	**Baserunning**	**Sliding**
Bat selection	Sacrifice bunt	Running mechanics	Bent-leg slide
Positioning in the box	Drag or surprise bunt	Exiting the batter's box	Pop-up slide
Stance and setup	Fake bunt	Running through first base	Headfirst slide
Timing and loading	Squeeze bunt	Braking	Hook slide
Swing mechanics	Push bunt	Rounding bases	Backdoor slide
Tracking		Leading off bases	Breaking up double plays
Pitch recognition		Tag-up	
Adjusting		Getting out of a rundown	
Hit and run		Heads-up running	
		Stealing	
		Dive backs	

Defensive			
Outfield	**Infield**	**Pitchers**	**Catchers**
Mechanical	**Mechanical**	**Mechanical**	**Mechanical**
Stance	Ready stance	Split step	Signal stance
Split step	Glove position	Pitch mechanics	Receiving stance
Perfect fly-ball technique	Triangle glove work	Hide ball and grips	Giving signals
Drop steps and back on fly	Backhand plays	Hit targets	Target
Drop steps and angle to grounder	Charging	Release point	Receiving the ball. Soft.
Lateral and crossover steps	Forehand and side plays	Fielding bunts	Throwing hand position
Catching below waist	Setting feet	Cover third on bunt	Position in box
Throwing technique	Throwing technique	Backing up bases	Getting to throwing position
Charging	Fielding bunts and slow rollers	Reaction fielding	Blocking balls
Do-or-die grounders	Catching pop-ups	Covering home on PB and WP	Footwork on throw
Hitting cutoff	Setting up for pitch, split step	Tags	Surround the ball on bunts
Ball straight over head	Moving with pitch	Pop-up communication	toes to the line
Run to spot on gapper	Rundowns	Catching pop-ups	both hands down on pickup
Backing up outfielders	Rundown throws	Fielding off the mound	Pitch out
Backing up infielders	Flips	Throwing to bases	Dropped 3rd strike
GB take a knee	Cut and relay throws	Footwork on throw	Pickoffs
Diving and sliding catches	Force outs—stretch, footwork	Delay steal	body position
RF throws to 1B	Tag plays	First-and-third defense	throw tech/location
Sac fly fake catch	Footwork on pickoffs	Rundowns	Intentional walk
	Barehanded play		Tag plays
Mental	Diving	**Mental**	Blocking the plate
Communication	All throws	Get ahead and stay ahead	Passed ball tech and communication
Pop-up coverage and talk	Slap defense	Pitch goals	

Defense

Runner on first base
Runner on second base
Runners on first and second base
Runners on first and third base
Rundowns, all bases
Bunt and run
Double steal
Relays

1B	2B	SS	3B
Base footwork	Pivots	Pivots	Surround bunts
Pickoffs	Covering first on bunt	Covering second on pickoff or steal	Diving
Surround bunts	Covering first on pickoff	Covering third on pickoff or steal	Pickoffs
Snap throw	Covering second on pickoff or steal	Talk with 3B and 2B each pitch	Suicide bunts
Short-hop throws	Relay responsibilities		
Use bag for high throws	Force footwork at first and second		
Footwork to the bag	Heads-up pickoff		
Glove flips	Angle footwork		

Game situation—score, inning, and so on	Know the umpire	Cutoff communication	
Positioning	Communication with catcher	1-3 plays/technique	
Know all pitches and likely outcomes	Pitch with a plan	Rundown technique	
Check field and conditions	Visualize	Returning the ball to pitcher	
Know foul and dead-ball area	Routine—work confidence	Up the line 100% with no runners on	
Anticipate hit	Use pregame to know hitters when possible		
Wind, sun, and grass	Use warm-up effectively		
Check fence and warning track	Check out the mound area		
Know runners' and batter's speed	Nonstarters know possible role and warm-up needs		
Know teammates' strengths	Throw all pitches early in the game		
When not to catch a foul ball	Between-inning meetings with coach and catcher		
	Consistent mechanics, no tipping		

Mental
- Test foul lines before the game
- Check out backstop/plate area
- Communication with umpire respectful and courteous
- don't turn your head/show him up
- Communicate with a pitcher
- Know pitchers' strengths
- Know hitters' strengths
- Use warm-up effectively
- Mound communication
- Know the situation
- Get ahead of batter
- Make sure fielders are in position
- Meet between innings with pitcher and coach
- Get scout info on opponents if available
- Throw all pitches early in game
- Know obstruction rules
- ACT like a leader

Mental

Visualization pregame	Know runners' and batter's speed	All pitch signals	Backup responsibilities
Field conditions—wet, fast, slow	Defensive signals	Watch batter's hands, know mechanics	Read ball off the bat
Sun, wind factors	First-and-third defense	Check base coaches for signs	Call steals
Foul ground	Pickoff coverage	Infield fly rule	Know score, inning, situation
Foul lines—roll ball	Communicate with outfielders	Know batter's history, pregame scouting	Communication
Depth of position	Know pitcher and possibilities		

Game Etiquette

Rules of the game	Between innings infield warm-ups	Personal gear	Keep dugout neat
Game management and structure	Between innings outfield warm-ups	Bench responsibilities	Pay attention to the game
Sprint on and off the field	Between innings pitcher and catcher warm-ups	Shagging foul balls	Equipment setup
Courteous to umpires	Gloves and hats while we are at bat		

Full Body

During this time our players go through a specific dynamic warm-up that is designed to get their bodies warmed up in softball-specific ways and ready to attack the practice both physically and mentally. A few examples are arm circles (to warm up the shoulder joints), high skips, sideways shuffles, and walking lunges.

Arm Care

Over the course of a full season, players' arms get a lot of use. Taking a proactive approach to arm care can help prevent arm injuries before they occur. Our players each have an elastic band that they attach to a fence. They then perform a variety of arm-strengthening and activating exercises including front raises, side raises, front and rear flys, and internal and external rotations.

Catch, Throw, Receive

Arm warm-up is a great time to reinforce proper mechanics and attention to detail. We call it catch, throw, receive to reinforce the concept that even though we're warming up, we're still practicing important aspects of the game. Our players go through an established throwing routine that ensures they're properly warmed up as well has them practice all the various types of throws and receiving patterns they'll see in the game. We also include a long-toss program to build arm strength.

Defense

At this point in practice, we typically progress into softball-specific skills, beginning with defense. With the defensive portion, we want to progress from simple to more complex. On a daily basis we begin with the simplest elements of defense, get in a high number of repetitions, and then practice that specific skill in a live or randomized environment.

Daily Skills Repetition

Another great opportunity to reinforce skill development and attention to detail is daily skill repetition, which we call prepractice fundamentals, or PPFs for short. We have a few versions of this that we cycle through; a sample of two different days of PPFs is shown in table 2.2. Cycling through different versions keeps it fresh while still hammering away at the daily skill development that is crucial to our sport.

Small Skills Groups

This part of practice is typically broken down into the following groups: middles, corners, pitchers, catchers, and outfielders. Here we really start to focus on covering new skills or brushing up on old ones. A typical small skills segment might have our middles practicing double-play footwork, corners practicing catching balls at the fence, catchers working on blocking,

Table 2.2   Prepractice Fundamentals Chart

Day 1	Day 2
Catch, throw, receive basics	Catch, throw, receive basics
Throws	Abbreviated throws
• All throws	Throws on the run
Infield	Drop step
Ground balls	Drop step running catch
Forehands to all angles	Lateral crossover with running catch
Backhands to all angles	Forward step, no false step
Short hops—straight on, forehand, backhand	Slide catches
	Shoestring catches
Slide dives	Tags: keep hands home, tag base not runner
Flips and feeds	Over right shoulder
Shovels	Over left shoulder
Catchers	Wraparound
Blocking	Drop and up
• Breakdowns	Sweep
• Shadows	Sell
Framing	Glove flips
Pop-ups	
Balls at fence	
Bunt footwork	

pitchers working on pop-ups, and outfielders working on catching balls at the fence. Depending on the day, we'll do anywhere from one to three small skill groups. We limit these sessions to 10 to 15 minutes. This activity is simply a quick opportunity to get some repetitions and brush up on skills.

Bigger Skills Groups

At this point in practice we put together a larger group to work on integrating several positions. We might do left side and right side; one coach hits tweeners or pop-ups to the left side (LF, SS, 3B, P) and another hits to the right side (RF, CF, 2B, 1B). Another example would be infield working on bunt coverage and outfield working on communication on balls in the gaps. We also frequently use this time to get a lot of repetitions, both ground balls and fly balls.

Live

This section is an opportunity to work on full-field defense. Out of season or early in the year, we practice full-field fungo, moving from no runners to live runners. During this time we incorporate all decision-making elements of the game—cuts and relays, situations, secondary plays, and so on.

We also use this time for our players to work on their baserunning decision making. As our players become settled into their positions, we continue to increase both the speed of the game and the pressure of the situation. As an example, we might practice our 2.6 defense with no outs and runners at first and third. In this scenario the base runner at home starts farther up the line to mimic a 2.6 home-to-first runner. Our players have to react to both the ball and the runners to make a quick decision.

Read-and-React Softball

An important aspect of coaching our sport is to encourage read-and-react softball. The issue has been discussed often in softball circles in recent years—kids don't play sandlot ball anymore. From an early age they take lessons in throwing, hitting, pitching, conditioning, and so on. And all of their team practice is done under the watchful eye of a coach. Although the coaches are usually well intentioned, players are inevitably told when, where, and how to throw the ball. They don't learn to read the situation, gauge the speed of the runner, know their own arm strength, and from all of those factors (and others) make a decision on what to do with the ball. Because of these factors, I believe that an important aspect of coaching is to encourage and push players to understand how to read and react. We do many drills that teach players how to read the pace of the ball, how to see a play breaking down, how to anticipate secondary plays that can happen after a broken play, and much more. As players become more comfortable with decision making, we increase the speed of each drill to put more mental pressure on the players. The intent is to make game day feel easy. We want them to celebrate that day and know that they're prepared for anything that the game will throw at them. They also know that even if they haven't practiced a particular situation, they understand how to diagnose it and make a decision on the fly. Of paramount importance in a read-and-react system is a coach's willingness to tolerate mistakes. Players will make mistakes, but they will also learn and grow from them. Ultimately, we want the players to take ownership—of their growth, the game, and their careers.

As with coaching the read-and-react component, we always try to coach a competitive aspect. We want our players to learn to embrace and seek out the pressure of competition. To do that, pressure needs to be normalized for them. They need to know that the pressure of competition is something they can use as a positive force rather than a negative burden.

Pitching

Although pitchers are a part of the defense, they merit a section to themselves. Because pitching is highly individualized, our first preference is to do our bullpens either before or after practice. Pitchers can get ground ball repetitions and hit (if they're hitting pitchers) during practice, and our catchers can be fully involved in practice. Occasionally we have to schedule the bullpens during practice, usually during the offensive segment. Catchers either rotate through (to allow them to hit) or get in extra cuts after the bullpen.

As with defense, we try to begin with the end in mind. Approximately where do we want the pitchers to be in terms of stamina, execution of pitches, mental game, and so on by the first game? We then reverse engineer their practice schedule from that end point. For each pitcher, we plan several weeks in advance the days when she'll be throwing bullpen, the days that are live, her rest days, and the focus points for each week. The schedule is flexible because a pitcher may need an extra off day or live day, but the overall system provides structure to both the coaches and the players. Besides programming the days, we also plan the general aspects we'll be working on—intentional walks, working to get ahead, specific mechanical or pitch focuses, and so on.

Offense

All too often in an offensive segment you see one player hitting, perhaps another player on a tee, and 12 to 15 other players standing around and shagging. With a little planning and thought, offensive practice can go from lots of standing around and shagging to a highly efficient, high-repetition segment of practice.

We begin with a hitting warm-up, which generally entails a line of tees along one foul line. Each player hits 5 to 10 balls at each of several locations—high inside, high outside, low inside, low outside. In addition, they often finish off the tee work with one or two drills that either address something they're working on or focus them on what we'll be working on that day. After they've warmed up their swings and are mentally prepped to hit, we move into front toss, batting practice, live, or some combination of those options. For front toss, we usually set up double front toss on the main field—two coaches throwing batting practice behind nets with several large screens dividing the two hitters and protecting the coaches. One coach throws inside and the other outside, or drops and rises, or any combination needed. From there the players rotate in pairs into one or two shag stations, standing in on a pitcher's bullpen, tee work, player front toss, bunting station, and an on-deck station. An important side note about player front toss is that safety is a key aspect, so players need to wear helmets and understand how to throw properly from behind a screen. This practice is a good default option because it provides a lot of reps in an efficient manner. If we're working either full batting practice (situations, such as a coach imitating a pitcher we'll face) or live, then we put a full defense on the field and usually have the players in groups of three to have base runners within each group.

When working batting practice or live, many options are available. For example, for the RBI drill, a player starts at second base and her partner has to hit her in with a 0-0 count. Or you can use a defined rotation with situations. In this type of drill, one partner starts at first base. In round 1, the hitter might sacrifice bunt her to second base, push bunt her to third, and squeeze her home. In round 2, the player executes a hit and run to second, hits opposite field to third, and hits a deep fly ball to score her partner. You can change up the options depending on your focus for that day.

When planning the offensive side of practice, be sure you don't neglect the mental side of hitting. We work not only to get our players better on a technical and mechanical level but also to improve their mental state of mind with discipline drills, pressure drills, and failure recovery drills. Much of this topic links back to the growth mind-set concept touched on earlier. One part of this concept is continually praising our players for having a great approach, rather than praising for outcome. In drill form, an example is making an adjustment between swings. If a player pops up, she simply has to do something different—hit a line drive, a grounder, or even miss completely as long as she is on top of the ball. If she is able to do that, we count it as a successful at-bat.

We also put our players in tough high-pressure situations to teach them how to embrace the moment and have no fear of failure. An example might be a game of 21 outs; the team has to get 21 outs in a row with no errors or mental mistakes. If they make a mistake, they start back over at 0. They'll feel the pressure build over the course of the outs and will become more accustomed to that pressure over time.

Staffing

At lower-division tiers of the game, coaches don't always have the luxury of multiple (or any) assistants or student managers. If this scenario applies to you, I encourage you to try a couple of different avenues. Seek out volunteers. You often don't know what help can be provided until you ask. I once had a semiretired coach as my volunteer assistant, and he was invaluable. He enjoyed the opportunity to give back and stay connected with the sport, and I loved having a second set of hands at practice and games. If you're unable to get any help I encourage you to teach the players to coach each other. This option is more time consuming on the front end as you teach each player what to look for at specific stations or drills, but it can pay dividends down the road. Although they certainly won't be able to teach at the same level you can, having 12 to 18 sets of eyes working to help each other improve is better than having just one set of eyes. If you do choose to enable your players, I encourage you to pick out one or two key aspects that you want them to focus on rather than overwhelm them with a variety of teaching cues. You'll often find that a bonus effect occurs—your players will better understand how to perform the skill because of having to teach it.

Time of Year

Time of year is an important factor to consider when planning practice. The seasons should all have a different focus.

Down Time

Focus: Rest and Recover

At the conclusion of our season we always take at least two to three weeks off from all activity except rehab and recovery. For another two weeks after that we encourage strength and mobility work as well as a return to activity (NCAA rules do not allow college coaches to mandate summer workouts, but we provide optional workouts for our players) and encourage a gradual reentry to skill work. Players need true downtime both to allow the body to recover and to prevent mental fatigue. If you coach younger players, encourage them to play multiple sports and take planned breaks from softball. This approach will be a benefit to them in the long run.

Off-Season or Fall Season

Focus: Individual Improvement

Off-season is the best time to break down mechanics or technique. When you teach any new skill, players go through the phases of learning, specifically through what is referred to as a conscious competence learning model. In this model players go from unconscious incompetence (the player is either unaware of the skill or simply unaware of her own skill level), to conscious incompetence (awareness of the fact that she doesn't possess the skill), to conscious competence (still thinking about the skill but able to perform it), and finally to unconscious competence (she doesn't have to think about the skill to perform it at a high level). Remember that in the second and third phases, performance often suffers a temporary setback because performance of the new technique is uncomfortable and still disjointed. As the player becomes more proficient at the skill, performance will certainly improve. Taking on the challenge of learning a new skill or progressing in an old one is much easier if the player knows that she won't be called on to perform in the near future. With that template in mind, off-season is the time to work in smaller groups, break down technique (great time for lots of video work), and work to become a better, more complete player. Rarely, if ever, do we do any kind of mechanics overhaul in season or even in preseason, because it takes too long for players to progress to that unconscious competence phase where the skill feels natural and comes easily.

Preseason

Focus: Team Improvement

Preseason is when all the individual skills work begins to be put consistently toward a team focus. We implement our schemes in more detail and make sure we're polished on all the team aspects—bunt coverage, first-and-third plays, relays, and so on. Our hitters rarely make any big mechanical changes to their swings and are now working on repetitions and timing. During this time our pitchers, depending on how many are on the team, throw anywhere from one to three times live during the week, in addition to bullpens.

As efficiently and quickly as we can, we get into live and situational work at game speed. A primary goal for our staff is to push the pace of practice and drills to the edge of our players' abilities. Ideally, on game day we want our players to feel that the game is moving at a slower pace than practice, that the game is easier than practice.

In Season

Focus: Continuous Improvement

In season our focus is on staying sharp, polishing up any issues we noticed from our last game, and preparing for our next opponent.

Staying Sharp

To stay sharp, we make sure that we consistently work on our fundamentals, on doing the little things the right way. We continue with our skill fundamentals segments throughout the season. As the long season carries on, I find this to be an area where coaches really have to focus because it can be tempting to let good enough slide by. The behaviors we allow are the standards we set. If we allow our team to slip in subpar focus, intensity, or attitude, then we're effectively telling them that our standard for them is lower than that of championship behavior.

Polishing

Nothing highlights our weaknesses as well as a strong opponent. We welcome strong opponents because they let us know exactly where we need to have a laser-like focus on improvement, and they help prepare us for postseason play. As a coaching staff, we sit down after every game and highlight the one or two priorities for improvement that we saw in the game. We then share those with the team at our first practice so that they're mentally prepared to work on them in the first one or two practices of that week.

Preparing

By midweek, after we've polished up any areas of improvement from the last game, we start to turn our attention to our next opponent. After we've decided how to prepare for that team, we add elements of our game plan to focus on in practice—how we're going to defend their better offensive players, how we want our pitchers to attack their hitters, how we want to attack their pitcher in the box, and so on.

For our final practice of the week, after we've covered areas of improvement as well as the upcoming opponent, we make sure that our players are mentally locked in for the game. We get them some reps to make sure they feel prepared and ready to attack, and then we have some fun.

Postseason

Focus: Confidence in What Got Us Here

When we reach postseason, everyone starts fresh. Postseason is an opportunity to celebrate what makes our team great, and we zero in on capitalizing on those strengths. As tempting as it may be, other than performing a general cleanup of all skills, I encourage you not to work to shore up your team's weaknesses in the postseason. You typically don't have enough time to make any big changes, and attempting to do so will often leave your players focusing on the negative of what they don't do well rather than the positive of what got them to the postseason in the first place.

The Fun Zone

In my experience, if you want your players to become their best version of themselves and rise to the occasion, you must do two things. You must first motivate them to be autonomous in the pursuit of excellence. Second, you need to make sure they have fun. The saying, although cliché, is true—it's a game and it should be fun. We try to incorporate some version of fun in every practice. Often the fun stuff is a competitive drill that serves the dual purpose of having fun and getting the competitive juices flowing. On some days we may just add a fun aspect to practice—practicing a home run trot, having a home run derby off a tee, and so on. Getting the players loose and enjoying themselves on a consistent basis usually has a positive effect on their mental state in practice and games.

Attitude and Mind-Set

An important aspect of any productive practice is each coach's mind-set, especially the head coach's. Early in my coaching career I found it easy to blow up in anger if a player didn't do exactly as I thought she should or if a play didn't go as expected. To be frank, it was an ego issue. I thought that flawed play negatively reflected on me as a coach, and I was impatient for my players to get it right. I needed a few years of maturing, as well as the counsel of some far wiser coaches, to help me see that my attitude in those moments was counterproductive to the ultimate goal of helping the team play at their best. Before each practice I strive to set aside any frustrations of the day or the past game and give my players my best during the few hours I have with them. We also have an accountability system in place with our staff; if one of us is having an off day, one of the other coaches pulls the person aside and reminds her or him to do a quick internal check and reset.

Mistakes

On a related note, how we as coaches deal with mistakes can send an important message to our players. We have a few nonnegotiables on our team, and one of the big ones is effort. If my players make a mistake or an error at full effort, we are committed to continuing to encourage them in that moment. The reality is that the vast majority of players want to do things the right way—they're certainly not *trying* to screw up. When I blow up after a player screws-up, I send the message that the outcome is the most important thing and that mistakes are never allowed. But I want my players to have zero fear of failure on the field. For that to happen, I have to reward the process of going 100 percent and be okay with some mistakes along the way.

Final Thoughts

We've discussed in the preceding pages many aspects of planning and organizing, which are important aspects of a successful program. As you plan and prepare for practice, I encourage you not to overscript practice. Although being detailed in planning the overall structure is important, ultimately our game is one in which the players need to be able to read and react to a variety of factors—the speed and direction of the ball, the speed of the runner, their own arm, the elements, and other factors. I encourage you, especially in live components, to spend less time dictating exactly where your players need to position themselves, throw the ball, and so on, and have them work to read those various factors and react in the moment. This approach comes with its share of mistakes, but ultimately it leads to smarter, better, and more engaged ballplayers.

Chapter 3

Incorporating Technology and Practice Tools

Beverly Smith

The essential equipment needed for softball and the Xs and the Os of the game have not changed much over the years. But the sport has changed in the area of technology. Technology can be found and applied in all areas of the game at a variety of price points. Examples include computerized pitching machines that can throw sequences of pitches, software that allows a coach to manage team rosters and calendars online, and applications for cell phones that give athletes video feedback. An effort to research the benefits and costs of technology that can improve your program is time well spent.

Today's athletes do not know life without the Internet or cell phones; they are connected 24/7 to technology. Using technology allows the coach to engage athletes and continue the learning process. My purpose is to introduce you to new ideas and tools to enhance your ability to communicate with today's athletes. To communicate effectively, you must be able to deliver your message to all types of learners. Challenge yourself to consider viewing both technology and training tools as additional vehicles to deliver the message. Over the years my coaching lessons are eerily similar, but my methods of teaching and communicating with the athlete continue to evolve.

Today's generation of athletes is visual, and the adage "A picture is worth a thousand words" is more applicable than ever. Consider communicating with your team in the medium that they are most familiar with: Instagram, Twitter, or group text. People have often said that if coaches can't get their message across in 140 characters (the maximum number of characters in a tweet), they shouldn't say it because they have already lost their audience. Coaches can establish a Facebook page and post team information, videos, and pictures as well as motivational messages. Video from practices and games can be a positive teaching tool. One way to share video with your team is with Dropbox, an easy online file-sharing program that allows multiple users to share folders. You can drop a specific video clip of a game-winning hit, huge strikeout, or ESPN-worthy defensive play in a player's folder for her to review after a game, or you can put game highlights for the entire team to review in a shared folder.

Many people are using Google Docs to be productive, creative, and collaborative. You can take the standard evaluation sheet that you have used for years and send a link to the players that will allow them to answer your questions online. Imagine the uses: You could request equipment sizes, survey the team for their favorite food, administer a softball rules test, and have all the data the players input immediately online. Google Docs is easy to learn; tons of online tutorials and YouTube videos can guide you through the process. Another idea in using technology with your team is to use their cell phones—they each have one. Have the players set a daily reminder or alarm on their phones. The phone will remind the player of the personal goal she set or what she wants to accomplish. The reminder might be to take extra ground balls, do 10 push-ups, or drink more water. In addition, a motivational message could appear on their phones each day.

Utilizing Video

The access and availability of video is the biggest change in technology. You can take high-quality video at practice with your cell phone or tablet. Multiple inexpensive applications are available for swing analysis. Simply download a swing analyzer app and get started. Being able to record from your smart phone or tablet allows you to give instant feedback to the athlete. Today's athletes are eager for technical feedback. The visual feedback is tremendous; you can draw on the screen and move the video image in slow motion. Some of the apps even allow you to save the video and e-mail the clip to your athlete. Other apps include advanced features that allow you to compare your athlete's swing against the swing of a professional player.

As a coach, you have the opportunity to video and analyze anything you want in a practice or game setting. My personal philosophy is to use the video to show and reinforce the aggressive cut at the plate, the successful swing, the excellent job with a drop step in the field, the perfectly timed steal, or the great frame or location of a pitch. My preference is for the athlete to see and repeat the positive images in her mind. If an athlete is struggling and needing to make technical adjustments, you should use the video for your benefit and then work on the problem with the athlete. You need to decide how much video to watch and how technical you need to be for your level of play. Be aware of paralysis by analysis; too much video can lead to overthinking, and the athletes can get lost in the weeds with the detail. Ideally, you want to coach your players to be relaxed and focused, to be reacting and playing the game. Video can give athletes a confidence boost when they see themselves doing things correctly. Confidence for the female athlete is half the battle; using video positively can have a huge effect. Consider making a confidence-booster video for each player. Take multiple clips of a player's great swings and put it on loop for a positive swing affirmation video. Do the same for pitchers with swings and misses and let that positive video replay in their minds.

On game days, having a video set in center field (offset of the pitcher) zoomed into the strike zone is helpful for postgame evaluation. You are able to view both the strike zone and each player at bat. Being able to look into the strike zone is an excellent way to evaluate the pitcher's game and the execution of each pitch. If possible, provide an extra copy of the game and strike zone for the continuing education of the umpire.

Tip: When viewing video on a PC, how can you view clips in slow motion?

Right Click, Enhancements, Player Speed Setting

Click arrows to advance frame by frame. Video is not only for hitting. The video shot from behind home can be used to evaluate team defense. The video helps give the athletes a visual of the positioning of defensive plays, base coverages, and backups. Players are always amazed at their timing as base runners. Being able to see the video of the pitcher's release in conjunction with the timing of the base runner's departure from the bag is always eye opening for the athletes. As the coach, you have to decide what information is relevant and important for you and your program. Do you have two video cameras? Do you have the staff to run both? What will you do with all the information?

Tip: Don't forget extra batteries, extension cords, a shower cap for your camera, and a backup power source. Being prepared with a contingency plan is always important!

Besides its usefulness for skill evaluation, video can be a great teacher. College softball is readily accessible through nationally televised games. Pay attention to outstanding plays in games that you watch and let your players learn from the best in the country. Note the outstanding baserunning, excellent sacrifice bunting technique, and examples of situational hitting. You can even use examples of plays to explain rules to your players and improve their softball IQ. Saved video lessons always make for a useful classroom session on a rainy day. The ESPN Watch App give you access to a plethora of games.

Scouting Opponents

Technology can also be used to prepare your team for game day in several other areas. Video has made scouting opponents much easier. If conference rules allow, consider filming the opposing pitchers. Video of the opposing pitcher from behind home plate can familiarize your team with the pitcher's windup and timing. You may be able to pick up a tendency on a specific pitch or a different grip that your hitters can identify. Ultimately, if your hitters have seen the pitcher and are familiar with her windup, they will be able to make quicker adjustments in the game. How you scout opponents and the information you want to obtain varies for all programs. Are statistics available for your league or conference? What tendencies or weaknesses does the batter have? In the past you could obtain hitting tendencies by going back and reading the play-by-play account in games and making a chart for each hitter. Of course, you can still do that today, but collegiate coaches can now subscribe to scouting services. These services take the online data and export it into convenient charts of hitter tendencies. In the past coaches gave signals using body parts. Pitching coaches signaled in the pitches using numbers or touches on the face and body. Now athletes commonly wear signal cards on their arms to dummy proof all offensive and defensive signs. You can purchase a software program that prints out signal cards for every game. An inexpensive way to make signs pick proof is to make your own cards on an Excel sheet and have your own system to chart hitter tendencies in the dugout.

Standardizing Data

One of the biggest pushes in technology is standardizing measurable data. These data are a key component in evaluations for recruiting and for student-athlete development. Today's athletes and coaches can benefit from the standardization. If you are a college coach you can use the data to analyze, monitor improvement, and motivate the achievement-minded athlete. Watching the measurable data improve year after year is empowering for the student-athlete.

What is measurable?
- Bat speed
- Overhand speed
- Pitch speed
- Foot speed
- Quickness in agilities
- Strength

Zepp (zepp.com/softball) is an example of cutting-edge software that uses technology to produce measurable data. Placed on the end of a bat, the Zepp chip has the capability to read bat speed, hand speed, impact angles, swing plane, and the time to impact. The software captures 1,000 points of data and is able to produce a 3D image of the hitter's swing. Both coaches and athletes can track progress, analyze the athlete's game, and note improvements. This method accelerates the learning process and measures improvement.

In the recruiting process, standardized measurable data take out the subjectivity. These data can help parents understand the athleticism of their daughter. For a high school or travel ball coach who deals with parents and manages the recruitment of student-athletes, the measurable data will be important to collect and use when communicating with college coaches. The testing of athletes at certified events where skills are measured and data are collected is becoming prominent in the recruiting process. If you are not able to have an athlete tested, you should do your best to provide college coaches with accurate data on your athlete's measureable skills.

Organizing Opportunities

Most coaches do not have video departments, an army of managers, or a large staff to implement all the advancements. But the overwhelming benefit of technology is that it allows coaches to be more efficient and affect multiple areas of their programs. It is well worth the time to research the cost of software or online programs that allow you to use multiple platforms under one roof. Consider the ability to distribute information to parents, athletes, and fans, manage the roster, manage the master calendar, score the games, post statistics, and even stream the games live. The portability and size of video cameras make it easy to attach the device to a chain link backstop and stream the game. The ease and availability of the technology gives the coach the opportunity to build the fan base; parents and fans can watch games from computers at work. All this certainly lends itself to multiple fund-raising opportunities. Have you considered enlisting a student to be the "voice of the (insert mascot)" and broadcasting the games on the Internet? That experience could be valuable for a student outside softball at your school. Many online programs offer one-stop shopping in terms of full administrative management for your softball program.

Essential Equipment

Along with various technologies to consider for your program, a lot of equipment is needed to run an effective practice at any level. Table 3.1 is a checklist of the essential equipment for any softball program.

When applicable, a drill for the training tool or product is included. Being listed in the chapter is not an endorsement of one product over another; in

Table 3.1   Equipment List for Practices

Offense	Defense	Pitching	Catching	Field management
Tees	Balls*	Nine-zone net	Chest protector*	Paint or chalk
Mirrors	Shag buckets	Radar gun*	Helmet*	Rakes*
Nets	Small gloves	Spinner	Shin guards*	Drag mat
Specialty balls (varying sizes)	Cones	Rev spin		Fence toppers
Practice and game balls*	Speed ladders	Batting dummy		Safety equipment*
Pitching machine*	Extra bases and pitching rubber	Balance beam		Tape measure*
Helmets*	Equipment for indoor practice	Weighted balls		Wall pads
Equipment for indoor practice		14-inch (36 cm) balls		
Screens and nets*		Power cord		
Throw-down plates				
Bats*				
Specialty bats				

Technology	Coach, administrative	Arm care and speed training	Resources	Program
Right View Pro	Lineup cards*	Surgical tubing	NFCA.org	Concessions
Dartfish	Rule book*	Ladders	NCAA.org	Tickets
iScore	Substitution, DP/ flex rule	Warm-up routine*	eligiblitycenter.org	Parking
Video camera	Stop watch*		softballexcellence. com	Program communication
Tripod, spider grips	Umpire rule book		Mentor	Fund-raising
Send info to team	Clipboard			Internet broadcasting
Tablet or iPad	Scorebook			Video streaming
Stat program	Signal cards			Scoreboard
Coaches Eye App	Charts			Sound system
	Seeds and gum			
	Visor			
	Sunscreen			
	First-aid kit*			
	Emergency contact list*			

* Absolutely essential equipment

fact, competing products are listed in each space for your review. Again, the purpose is to encourage you to consider new ideas for your program.

Balls

As you read the chapter you will note the numerous drills that can be created with various types of balls. Depending on space and setup for practice, having a variety of balls allows you to get your athletes more work or repetitions within practice.

Typical Balls to Use at Practice
- Softballs
- Baseballs
- Tennis balls
- Incrediballs
- Wiffle balls
- Lite Flite balls
- Machine balls
- 14-inch (36 cm) balls

Specialty Balls to Use at Practice
- Medicine balls
- Zip balls
- Muhl balls
- Footballs

Nothing is more important to infielders and outfielders than live balls off the bat, but ground-ball work can become monotonous. Here are some suggestions to challenge today's athlete and get focused repetitions using a variety of equipment during practice.

Baseballs

Try a defensive workout with baseballs. Baseballs speed up the game and place the focus on a smaller object. Zip balls are also fun because they are smaller than baseballs and will challenge the infielders.

Tennis Balls

Tennis balls can be used to replicate a bouncier hit. Fielders can execute with small gloves or by seeing the ball into their bare hand. The following specialty equipment works well with tennis balls.

Small gloves   keep players' focus on the ball and allow them to feel the ball with the hands.

Paddles   can be used for soft hands.

Foam pad with a strap on the back   keeps players from closing the glove too early and helps with transferring the ball to the throwing hand quickly.

Lite Flite Balls

These balls can be used to hit harder and at close range to test the athlete's reaction time.

Incrediballs

Incrediballs can be used to work short hops at the bases. Knowing that they won't get hurt, the athletes can challenge each other in practice with realistic short hops that they will have to handle in games.

Footballs

Basic footballs can help the athletes understand angles and the technique used to drop step and run. Emphasis can also be placed on running with the arms and extending for the ball for the catch.

Nets and Screens

Nets and screens are imperative to running a safe and efficient practice. Screens in the batting cage or on the field for front toss are vital for batting practice. Catch nets give you the ability to set up hitting stations anywhere, and they can double as targets for your defensive practices. Screens can be light, portable, and easy to travel with as well.

Bats

Besides having bats for practice and competition, coaches should consider specialty bats for training purposes. Table 3.2 outlines the uses and benefits of each kind of specialty bat.

Table 3.2   Uses for Specialty Bats

Type of bat	Benefit
Wood bats	Strength, bat speed, feel of sweet spot
Skinny bats	Eye–hand coordination, tracking to barrel, and swing accuracy
Youth tee ball bats	One arm and hand path
Wiffle ball bat	Feel of maximum bat speed and bat whip
Fungo bat	Barrel awareness

Tees

Having five or six tees gives a coach the ability to structure an efficient offensive practice. Throw-down plates for the tee stations are imperative for the athlete to understand positioning in the box and contact points.

Four Corner Tees

Setup

Set up two tees on opposite sides of the plate. One tee is at the top of the strike zone inside, and the other is at the bottom of the zone outside. After repetitions, switch tees to low and inside and high and outside.

Execution

Contact points need to be set for where the athlete sets up in the box. Up and in, low and out: Set a ball on each tee. The athlete always starts on the up tee. She executes the swing on the up tee and then executes the swing on the low tee. She repeats for round 1 and then switches with a partner. Players execute two or three rounds before moving the tees to high and out and low and in.

Coaching Points

This drill can be executed with various balls and set up in multiple locations at practice. Hitters will learn the size of the strike zone as well as how to handle both pitches, not just in and out. If your athletes are hitting the pitch correctly, they will not hit the alternating tee.

Pitching Machine

A pitching machine is an essential piece of equipment that offers several uses for a softball program. Primarily, a pitching machine facilitates repetitions for the athletes. A pitching machine gives you the ability to pitch to a specific zone or at a consistent speed. A pitching machine also can be used to produce challenging defensive plays for catchers and outfielders.

Three Plates

Setup

One machine, three throw-down plates set at 36, 40, and 43 feet (11, 12, and 13 m)

Execution

This drill allows the pitching machine to be set at one speed in one location. The athletes take three reps at each plate. As they progress from the front plate to the middle plate to the back plate, they focus on their timing to continue to hit the ball up the middle. This drill creates a perceived change of speed, so the hitters need to adjust their timing.

Coaching Points

An important part of the setup is to make sure that the pitch is a strike at each plate. The drill works best when the person feeding the machine gives a consistent windmill motion. Athletes need to recognize the differences in timing at each plate and identify when they need to start their load for each pitch.

Stopwatch

A stopwatch is an essential tool for any softball program. It provides important measureable data for the coach and student-athlete. With a stopwatch you can gather valuable information in practice or games. What is your catcher's pop time? Do you know how long it takes your left-handed slapper to reach first base from contact? How fast is your opponent's slapper or fastest athlete?

Game Speed Defense

Setup

Full defense; coach-controlled hits and bunts from home for slap or bunt defense

Execution

The coach stands with the stopwatch and presses start on contact from the batter or coach at the plate; the defense fields the ball and throws to first base. The coach presses stop when the ball is caught at first base. If the stopwatch reads less than three seconds, the coach yells, "Out." If the time is more than three seconds, the coach yells, "Safe." This drill is an excellent way for the defense to practice at a true game pace for players with speed.

Coaching Points

The defense works against the clock at game speed to prepare for a speed team and to understand work rate. Coaches need to determine speed for your level in times to first base.

Radar Gun

A radar gun is an essential tool in both practice and games for pitchers. In practice, the radar gun can be used in pitching workouts to observe pitch speed differential with the fastball and changeup. What is your pitcher's average speed? What is the speed of her changeup? Does she understand what she needs to do to throw the changeup consistently at that speed? During a game, monitoring a pitcher's speed allows you to identify whether she is fatiguing or gauge the pitch count at which she fatigues. The following checklist is a reminder of what you want to measure when using a radar gun.

Radar Gun Checklist

- Clock opponent's pitch speed
- Measure bat speed
- Measure overhand speed
- Check speed of pitching machine

Additional Tools

Many pitching tools and accessories are available on the market today. Again, my coaching philosophy is to be willing to try anything that will help my athletes better understand a concept, allow the pitcher to feel something, or create feedback for my pitcher. Today's pitchers crave feedback. The Spin Right Spinner and the 14-inch (36 cm) softball are two tools that receive rave reviews from my pitchers. Working with a Spinner allows the pitcher to see exactly how the center of the ball is spinning. It allows the pitcher to work on proper spin for various pitches. Similarly, the 14-inch ball provides excellent feel for the pitchers at release. After using the oversized ball, the regulation ball feels small and light in the pitcher's hand. For performance measures, the Rev Spin measures the spin rate on the ball. You can use it to evaluate pitchers and monitor their development and improvement.

You can try many options to serve as a batting dummy. Two stacked garbage cans can work, but if you have the budget, a bullpen session with the batting dummy in the box is valuable. It is a realistic visual aid for the pitcher. The pitcher can practice her pitches against a left-handed batter who is crowding the plate or against a right-hander who has moved to the back of the box. Several strike zone or nine-zone nets are available for pitchers to work a bullpen without a catcher.

Finally, to prevent overuse injuries, all coaches need to know how much their athletes are practicing and playing. Today's athletes play year round and do not give their bodies proper rest and recovery. Having a warm-up routine is essential for the prevention of injury. Implementing an arm and shoulder routine to your practices is useful for strengthening and prehabilitation. For a solid arm program that is self-explanatory and easy to implement, look up "Throwers 10" on the Internet.

Never be afraid to ask questions, seek a better idea, or learn something new. As an educator you should always be looking to grow as a coach and teacher of the game.

All coaches should have a network of information, mentors, and resources. Books, DVDs, YouTube videos, coaching courses, and coaching clinics are available everywhere. Don't limit yourself only to hitting and defensive drills for softball. Be on the lookout for resources dealing with the mental game, vision training, team-building activities, recruiting, leadership, and other applicable topics. Dive in and soak up what fits your personality and style and implement it into your program. Finally, don't forget that all coaches need a mentor. You need someone you can be honest with about the issues and challenges you face in your program. Having a mentor you can trust and receive advice from is extremely helpful to your professional growth. And, of course, if all else fails, Google it.

Resources

www.NFCA.org—National Fastpitch Coaches Association

www.NCAA.org—recruiting publications and information

www.softballexcellence.com—an example of the many websites that offer tips, drills, and current articles on softball

Chapter 4

Identifying Strengths and Weaknesses

Rachel Lawson

During the recruiting process, all coaches set out to identify the star player by evaluating her relative to the five tools—running speed, arm strength, hitting for average, hitting for power, and fielding. Through observation, coaches determine how each recruit will fit into a program based on her overall athleticism and the needs of the program. In addition, coaches frequently use an arbitrary sixth tool to identify a player's intangibles. In many circumstances, the identification and cultivation of this sixth tool define an athlete's strength and ultimate success in a highly competitive environment.

Power of the Mind

Each athlete is intrinsically motivated by different factors. By quickly identifying the source of the player's motivation, a coach can create a practice environment that nurtures immediate success. These successes help build the confidence necessary for the athlete to perform at her optimal potential.

Value

Value must be placed on what the athlete brings to the team. Two immediate questions help us better understand what that value is: What does the athlete add to the team? and What can she actually accomplish? The individual athlete often becomes distracted by placing too much value on what she does *not* bring to the squad or by fixating on her teammates' value instead of her own strengths. By simply focusing on what she can do, the athlete tends to become committed to perfecting that ideal. As a result, her true strengths become evident.

Breaking down the two basic questions can help us understand the type of value that the athlete possesses. The first question is, What does the athlete add to the team? Does the athlete play great defense? Does she have a strong arm? Does she have great leadership skills? Is she fast? Does she hit for a high average? Does she have a lot of power? Does she have great instincts for the game? Is she a supportive teammate?

The second question is, What can she actually accomplish? Can she mentally and visually adjust to the speed of the game at the higher level? Can she perform under increased pressure? For example, an athlete might be extremely fast but lack the offensive skills required to be successful at the higher pitch speeds. As a result, she will have a low on-base percentage and will be unable to use her speed. Another example is the incredibly strong athlete who is unable to use her strength because she strikes out too much. A final example is the teammate who is a supportive person by nature but may be unable to show this same attitude of teamwork if she is a bench player.

Often, players who place too much value on what they do not bring to the squad distract themselves from their own assets. In addition, athletes often become fixated on the values that their teammates may or may not bring to the team instead of focusing on their own strengths.

By simply concentrating on what she can do, the athlete tends to play with greater confidence and becomes more motivated to work at improving her skill set. By committing to perfecting that ideal, her true strengths become increasingly evident.

Confidence

Before people can succeed, they must first have confidence in what they are doing. At times, athletes fail not because they lack the ability to accomplish the specific goal but because they lack the confidence to get it right. Confidence can come from a number of sources including whether the player feels strong, whether she believes she is intelligent, whether she has acquired experience, whether she believes she is doing the right thing, and whether she has an identity that the team positively recognizes.

Success breeds confidence on and off the ball field. To have consistent success, an athlete must work hard all the time toward process-orientated goals. Working hard toward demanding goals and eventually achieving them tends to bring out the best qualities in most athletes. In addition, because a player is working incredibly hard at achieving her goals, she becomes consumed by her own abilities and does not have time to obsess about what others are doing. At this point, the athlete can gain self-awareness, which will eventually lead her to a better understanding about where her true strength lies.

There is no quick fix to obtaining sustainable confidence. Confidence is developed though patience and continued success.

Coaches should not rush to judgment about what players can and cannot do. When new players join the team, coaches immediately want to assess their strengths and weaknesses. But how a player reacts to her new environment often gives only a small glimpse of her true potential. A freshman may have the talent necessary to succeed but not the capacity to work as hard as her older, more experienced teammates. As a result, her natural strength is not instantly apparent. The younger athletes also need time and repetitions to gain the physical strength, maturity, and mental toughness necessary to adjust to the speed of the game.

A player needs time to acclimate to her new environment and adapt to a new coaching style and system. Likewise, the coach needs time to understand how each athlete best learns new tasks. The coach must also take into account that the speed at which the player will reach her actual potential is largely determined by how adaptable her mind-set already is. If the athlete is fixed on past successes, she might put in the time necessary to get better, but she will focus solely on the factors that created success in the past. If, however, the athlete focuses on the challenges that will allow her to conquer new obstacles, she will adapt to the speed and intelligence of the game at a much faster pace.

Only an athlete with high self-esteem and extreme mental toughness can show her true strengths when she is in an uncomfortable situation. Athletes who are pleasers are often difficult to assess accurately because they get bogged down in the small details and tend to perform poorly in new situations regardless of their innate skills.

Because of the many pitfalls when it comes to gaining confidence, fostering a steady environment that focuses on achieving success through working hard at mastering smaller process-oriented goals tends to bring to the surface more of each athlete's individual strengths.

Recognizing Self-Defeat

The most demanding practices should take place in the off-season or early in the preseason. During this period, the athlete needs to possess the coping skills necessary to endure demanding practices. In addition, she needs to trust that failing at a task is not an indictment on her value as a person; it is merely a measure of how she performed at a task at that specific moment. If the athlete does not possess the coping skills to perform difficult tasks, she will spiral out of control quickly. The environment will become negative and ultimately counterproductive because she will lose confidence and ultimately fail regardless of her athletic skill set. In addition, as she spirals downward, a few of her teammates may pull focus away from their own goals and focus on her failures, creating an even greater feeling of negativity.

When athletes do not feel good about what they are doing, they will not be as motivated and will likely underperform. A vicious cycle is created because the coach's job is to demand optimal performance. In many instances, instructions will be communicated through loud commands and assertive body language. Many people respond to this type of communication with an undercurrent of fear. And the normal response to fear is panic.

If negative thoughts and behaviors can be identified early, a coach can help pull the athlete out of this self-defeating mind-set. The challenges of the drills need to be conveyed in a manner that the athlete thinks that the goals are challenges that are fun to overcome.

Creating a Productive Environment

To prepare a team for the upcoming season, a coach must push the athletes to heights that they would not reach on their own. Well-planned goal setting that focuses on the five tools can be an effective instrument to use during the off-season to motivate athletes and to discover their strengths.

When setting goals, each individual goal should be both measureable and attainable. The purpose of setting smaller objectives is to allow each athlete to develop a task-orientated mind-set. By focusing on the smaller obtainable goals, the athlete will gain confidence with each success. After successfully achieving the standard, a newer and more difficult goal can be set.

A practical example illustrating this type of goal setting can be seen when working to improve a player's pop time. If a player is working on her overall pop time from the glove of the thrower to the glove of the receiver (glove to glove), the coach can break each component of the throw into smaller time increments. First, the coach records the length of time the player takes from catch to the point of release. While the coach is recording these times, the player can improve the techniques required to produce a quicker exchange. In addition, the coach records the amount of time from glove to glove. As the player's technique from catch to release improves, the player will find that her overall pop time will decrease. As the player becomes more efficient, the goal time from hitter's contact to catch and release can be steadily decreased. Specifically, we require our infielders to have the ability to field a ball hit by a slapper and throw it to first base in 2.6 seconds or less. When freshmen come into our program, their times are often much slower than 2.6 seconds. So, we generally set a much slower goal time of 2.9 seconds. As the athlete becomes more efficient, we set the goal time progressively lower until she eventually reaches the 2.6-second mark from hitter's contact to the putout.

This process of reaching and then creating a more challenging goal will show each player exactly where her strength lies. As the player learns to accomplish the set goals, the skills required to achieve the task will be seen as a strength. If the player is incapable of reaching the standard, the best option may be to remove her from that situation or at least minimize the importance of that skill relative to her overall value to the team to prevent her from losing confidence. The manner in which the coach chooses to remove the player from the situation is critical to tough player's overall development. If the coach chooses to yell across the field, the athlete may take the criticism personally and lose her productive mind-set. A better approach might be to pull the athlete aside and have a one-on-one conversation to explain why the results were not effective and what she needs to improve to see greater success. Another effective approach is to ask the player to come to practice a little early the next day so that she can work individually with a coach. This technique can be helpful because it removes the player from a potentially embarrassing situation where she will experience failure in front of a group. At the same time, the player sees that the coaching staff is invested in seeing her improve.

During the off-season, practice plans are focused on measuring and enhancing the strengths of each of the players' five tools—running speed, arm strength, hitting for average, hitting for power, and fielding.

The initial practices are designed to gain a baseline standard for each player's talent relative to the five tools. Gathering data on foot speed and arm strength is simple because each tool can be measured using a stopwatch. For an overhand throw, a radar gun can also be used. The standards identified for fielding ability and hitting for average and power are not as easy to collect in a practice setting unless statistics are gathered during live situations. In the case of the team's returning players, the statistics from the previous year can be used as a springboard for planning practice for the upcoming season.

After the baseline data are collected on each of the five tools, the player's fundamentals are analyzed using frame-by-frame video to determine whether specific mechanical adjustments can be made to develop the tool into a strength. Based on this determination, a long-term practice plan is developed that includes setting specific systematic goals that progress in difficulty throughout the entire off-season. By easing the athlete into the new system and allowing her to achieve and celebrate small successes en route to mastering more complex skills, the athlete will learn to enjoy the process of setting and ultimately achieving individual and team-orientated goals.

Traveling the Tough Road

People learn about themselves when they encounter difficult situations or tasks. If a player truly desires to get better, she must travel the tough road to get to her destination. By using isolated mechanical drills, situational drills, and live practice drills, coaches can design practice plans that work to build confidence in a more controlled environment and then steadily increase the difficulty of the tasks as the complexity and speed of the drills increase. As the drills become more difficult, an athlete's strengths and weaknesses will become glaringly obvious. Luckily, if the athlete possesses a positive mind-set, the willingness to work hard, and the toughness required to complete the challenges, she can get a little better at something each day. The key for most teams is to find what that something is so that it can be used on game day.

Isolated Drills

Countless isolated drills focus on individual mechanics. How a player performs under increased pressure often separates the players by strength in that skill set. During defensive workouts, a stopwatch can be used to manipulate the time required to accomplish the task. Other times, the range that must be covered to field the ball might be expanded.

During hitting, the coach can manipulate pitch speeds and introduce breaking pitches to put pressure on the hitter. A useful teaching technique that is often used has the younger athlete partnered up with a more experienced player in the hope that the younger player will try to catch the older player, mirror her initial success, and then ultimately surpass it.

Situational Drills

Situational offensive and defensive drills are also a great way to increase pressure during practice. When a player is put in various situations, she must be able to think about the play and then react accordingly. The players who do a better job of anticipating the play will have an advantage over those who are more reactionary, regardless of the players' innate strengths. If an athlete learns to pay attention, she can learn to anticipate better through preparation and repetition. An athlete who has great anticipation skills can be an effective teammate, but if she lacks innate skills in terms of speed and power, she will have a lower ceiling on the types of plays she can make.

Live Practice

Live practice is the best way to expose a player's strengths and weaknesses. Live situations should be fast paced and include multiple base runners. Hitters need to be able to react to pitched balls, defenders must be able to react to the depth and distance the ball is hit, and base runners must be able to read the trajectory of the ball off the bat and then react to the depth and distance of the batted ball.

Live situations expose players' strengths and weaknesses at a much faster pace than a practice plan that uses only isolated drills. Players who have great strengths will shine in these practices. On the other hand, if an athlete is incapable of performing during live sessions, the reason for her failure must be quickly identified. Did she fail because she lacks confidence? Did she fail because she lacked the experience to get it right? Is her failure a result of her inability to adjust visually to the faster pace and speed of the game? Or did she fail simply because she does not possess the skill set required to complete the task? After identifying the source of the failure, an individual plan can be implemented to place the focus back on isolated drill work that will help the athlete work through the process of reaching her destination.

A practical example of traveling the tough road can be seen in a younger right-handed hitter learning to hit the outside pitch to the opposite field. First, the hitter works on her offensive mechanics off a tee. After she masters driving the outside pitch to the right side of the field, she is progressed to short toss. During short toss, the hitter works on her mechanics while being asked to identify and attack only the outside pitch, taking all pitches thrown in other hitting zones. After mastering the mechanics needed to drive the outside pitch off short toss, the hitter is progressed to the pitching machine. Again, the hitter focuses on the mechanics of driving the outside pitch while the pitch is traveling farther and moving at much greater speed. After mastering hitting the higher-speed pitches, the athlete is put in a live batting practice (BP) situation off a practice pitcher. During this live BP, the hitter is asked to attack only the outside pitch, taking all other pitches including off-speed pitches. After gaining competency, the hitter is placed in situational hitting with a runner on second base. During situational hitting, the hitter focuses on driving the ball to the opposite field so that the runner on second will have a better opportunity to score.

Using Assessments to Facilitate Learning

The consistent use of players' and coaches' assessments serves as a powerful learning instrument that can help counsel the athletes and determine where strengths and weaknesses lie. Assessments work best when regularly scheduled meetings occur throughout the off-season. The first meeting should occur when practices first begin. During this assessment, the specific skills should be defined and baseline numbers should be taken. Next, a midseason assessment that includes new measurements should be taken to determine whether the athlete is on the right track. Finally, an assessment at the end of the off-season is scheduled to collect new numbers for the coaches and player to review and determine the athlete's progress.

To augment the process, a coach can create spreadsheets to rank the athletes on specific skills. The top 5 or 10 numbers can be posted in the locker room or distributed during a team meeting. Taking videos of the athletes excelling at the skills and showing them their success is both helpful and motivating.

Player Assessments

When scheduled on a routine basis, individual player meetings can help facilitate the learning process. During the process, a player should be required to assess her individual play in an objective manner, focusing on where she believes her strengths lie and where she can continue to work so that her weaknesses do not become team weaknesses. If handwritten assessments are also required of the athlete, she will be forced to think deeply about her skill set, which can help highlight obvious strengths and weaknesses. The coach should also fill out an assessment of the athlete. After both assessments are filled out, the coach and the athlete should schedule a meeting to discuss the results. During the meeting, the assessments indicate whether the player and coach are on the same page regarding the athlete's strengths. The assessments also serve as an objective form of communication that can improve the dialog between the coach and the athlete and make the learning process more efficient.

Table 4.1 is an example of a written player assessment that we use during individual meetings.

Coaches' Assessments

Coaches' assessments are an incredibly valuable learning tool if used consistently as a measure of where the athlete is at that moment. The use of video and statistical analysis accelerates learning because it removes a lot of player emotion from the learning process and places the mental focus on the task at hand. In addition, capturing a player's performance on video can enhance the speed of learning. By using statistics focused in smaller time intervals, checkpoints can be made to illustrate how much the player has improved in that designated period. Ideally, incremental jumps that show the player's strengths will occur, but if improvement doesn't occur, a player's weakness will be identified.

Competition

Competition often exposes an athlete's true character. The players who work hard to master their skills and have a greater sense of urgency tend to learn the game fast and are usually the better performers.

Without question, the teams that are the most prepared and understand where each player's strength lies have a stronger identity and an advantage over teams that are less prepared and lack understanding of what they are capable of doing well.

When game planning for the opposition, the team should always match their individual players' strengths against their opponents' perceived weaknesses. Information about the opponent can be collected before the game, during pregame, and during the game. The same instruments used to evaluate individual team strengths should be used to evaluate an opponent's strengths. Using a stopwatch, information can be gathered about arm strength and foot speed. When evaluating the opponent's pitcher, it is safe to assume that she is warming up her best pitches, spending more time

Table 4.1 Condensed Self-Evaluation

Defense						
Throwing—arm strength and carry	NA	P	F	G	VG	E
Throwing—accuracy	NA	P	F	G	VG	E
Throwing—speed of transfer	NA	P	F	G	VG	E
Fielding efficiency	NA	P	F	G	VG	E
Footwork—first step and angles	NA	P	F	G	VG	E
Glove work	NA	P	F	G	VG	E
Square range	NA	P	F	G	VG	E
Offense						
Hit for average	NA	P	F	G	VG	E
On-base percentage	NA	P	F	G	VG	E
Hit for power	NA	P	F	G	VG	E
Situational hitting	NA	P	F	G	VG	E
Short game	NA	P	F	G	VG	E
Approach (ahead in the count, with two strikes)	NA	P	F	G	VG	E
Speed	NA	P	F	G	VG	E
Decision making on the base paths	NA	P	F	G	VG	E
Mentality						
Ability to handle adversity (success under pressure, maturity, team player)	NA	P	F	G	VG	E
Bring your A game—consistency	NA	P	F	G	VG	E
Body language, composure	NA	P	F	G	VG	E
Coachability—retention	NA	P	F	G	VG	E
Competitiveness—tenacious physically and mentally	NA	P	F	G	VG	E
Health—injury prone	NA	P	F	G	VG	E
Kinesthetic awareness	NA	P	F	G	VG	E
Knowledge of the game	NA	P	F	G	VG	E
Unyielding approach—desire	NA	P	F	G	VG	E
Work ethic—consistency	NA	P	F	G	VG	E
Key: NA = not applicable, P = poor, F = fair, G = good, VG = very good, E = excellent						

From National Fastpitch Coaches Association, 2016, Practice perfect softball (Champaign, IL: Human Kinetics).

focusing on the ones that she believes bring her the most success. Opposing hitters often expose the weaknesses in their swings when they are in the on-deck circle or during the game based on where they are standing in the batter's box.

Softball, when played at the highest level, is a sport in which information about a player's strengths is gathered repeatedly and then used to make immediate in-game adjustments. The following example of an in-game scenario will be diagrammed to illustrate the individual adjustments that can be made by exploiting an athlete's strengths and weaknesses.

Examining an In-Game Situation

Here is an in-game scenario: The batter is a right-handed pull hitter, and the pitcher is a right-handed pitcher. The runner on second base has average foot speed, the count on the batter is 0-0, there is one out, and the game is tied 1-1 in the sixth inning.

The Batter

The batter steps in the box with her toes close to the batter's box chalk line closest to home plate. By positioning herself in this location in the box, she is communicating to the pitcher that she is trying to hit the outside pitch, that her strength lies in her bat speed, and that she believes she cannot be beat by an inside pitch.

The Pitcher

After recognizing that the batter is looking to hit an outside pitch, the pitcher knows that she must throw one of her best pitches on the inside part of the plate. The pitcher can also choose to throw some type of off-speed pitch to keep the batter off balance. If she throws an outside pitch close to the plate to get a strike on the batter, she risks giving up a hit because the hitter is communicating that she is attacking that zone.

The Fielders

By evaluating their opponent, the defense knows that this batter is a pull hitter and that the base runner's time from second to home will be roughly 5.8 seconds because she is of average foot speed. Each player positions herself on the field according to her arm strength and defensive range. Each outfielder starts at a distance from home plate according to her arm strength so that she can throw the ball home in a little less than 5.7 seconds. The infielders position themselves defensively so that they can keep the batted ball in the infield and get the out at first base.

The Base Runner

Because the base runner is at second, she will be able to see the flight of the pitched ball and the trajectory of the ball leaving the bat. Based on the knowledge she has gathered about her opponent's arm strengths and because she knows how fast she can run from second to home, she knows her likelihood of scoring on each type of hit based on the depth and distance that the ball travels off the bat.

Winning the Competition by Exploiting Individual Matchups

Assuming that over 200 pitches are thrown in an average college softball game, more than 200 different in-game scenarios can create matchups based on the players' individual strengths and weaknesses. The team that is better equipped to understand and create favorable matchups for their players will have a greater chance at winning on a consistent basis.

For a team to exploit individual matchups, they must first create a team culture during practice that brings to the surface each player's individual strengths. In addition, those strengths must be nurtured in an environment where they can be tested repeatedly in pressure situations so that the athlete can be better prepared to perform at her optimal level.

Imagine that you are playing your biggest conference rival in a winner-take-all contest. Your opponent's number 5 batter is at bat, and the count is two balls and two strikes. Because of scouting, your team's pitcher is aware that with two strikes, the batter is looking to hit an off-speed pitch up the middle. As a result, the pitcher throws a hard inside pitch that she has worked on in the bullpen on countless occasions, knowing that this ball will likely be hit to the right side of the infield. The batter swings but is late to hit the ball. As a result, she hits a ground ball to the second baseman close to the 3-4 hole. The second baseman is prepared to field the ground ball because she has been put in a number of high-pressure fielding situations at practice, including range drills in which she must have a pop time from hitter's contact to receiver's glove of 2.9 seconds. The result of the countless hours of skill mastery and preparation is an out.

If each teammate can recreate this defensive mind-set more than 100 times a game, the team will end up on the winning end of contests more often than on the losing side. Each contributing player will feel a sense of accomplishment not only for the win but also for all the hours and work she put in to master her skills. This confidence validates the team's process and promotes an atmosphere that is positive and will remain productive for many weeks to come.

Conclusion

Through careful evaluation during the recruiting process, a coach should work to determine a player's value relative to the five tools and at the same time assess the mentality that the player will bring to the field on a daily basis. After the player's strengths have been determined, she will have a greater chance of further developing her strengths in a positive, productive environment. The regular use of assessments is a helpful tool to determine whether the athlete is improving and to measure how she compares with the other athletes who play the same position. By continually mastering increasingly difficult tasks, the players will see their strengths become even stronger and will feel more confident and prepared for their upcoming competitions.

Chapter 5

Developing a Competitive Environment

Lisa (Sweeney) Van Ackeren

Athletes learn invaluable life lessons through their participation in sport. Exposure to competition on a public stage helps athletes learn how to handle pressure, recover from failure, and work with their teammates toward a goal. Setting up athletes for success on the public stage of a game begins with coaches who are dedicated to establishing a competitive environment for athletes to train and compete in. Building a competitive environment on a team can make everyone better if it's created in a way that promotes the success of all team members. The concept requires attention to detail and genuine concern for the development of all athletes on a team, but the result is a team that revels in the joy of competition and enjoys getting closer to their potential, individually and as a group.

The premise of this chapter makes an important and often unrecognized point about competitiveness: It can be developed. One of the dangerous assumptions a coach can make is that competitiveness is an innate quality. Either players have it or they don't. I'm sure that each of us is running through the rosters of seasons past (and present) and picking out those athletes who just don't seem to have it. But I believe that competitiveness can be taught to and enhanced in an athlete. This basic belief about competitiveness, whichever side of the issue you are on, drives the environment that you create when working with your teams during practice and in game situations. You should examine this within your own team environment to ensure that the coaching staff is getting through to everyone on the roster.

Assessing Competitiveness Within the Team

To build a competitive environment, the first step is to understand the current team culture. Here are a few questions to consider: What motivates this group of athletes? What three to five words most accurately describe this team? When presented with a challenge, how do they respond? What are our values as a team? This exercise can start among the coaches, but I encourage you to engage in a wider conversation with your student-athletes. Here is an example of how to engage the team in a culture-based conversation:

1. Group four or five athletes together, mixing classes, positions, and backgrounds.
2. Have them discuss the following topics in a group:
   a. Describe the best thing about this team.
   b. What makes us unique?
   c. What makes us championship worthy?
   d. What is our biggest challenge?
3. Engage in a full team discussion and have each group share a few thoughts based on the questions. Have a team member write down key points as you go. Play devil's advocate. A conversation should be occurring as a team rather than each group simply making their point.

The team often sees things a little differently than we as coaches do, and when it comes to culture, they are the primary creators, participants, and influencers of it.

After getting a handle on the unique culture of your team, a good next step is to evaluate all the environments that athletes are training in from the ground up. This list can include strength, conditioning, and agility sessions; individual lessons or workouts; small-group workouts; team practices; and games. To do this, I break the concept of competition up into two larger subtopics: competition within the team (athlete versus self, athlete versus teammates, and team versus practice) and outside competition (team versus the other guys).

Athlete Versus Self

Developing a competitive mind-set has to start within the athlete herself. One of the best ways to promote an athlete's competitive drive and her skill development is to set specific, tangible goals. At the close of our fall season, we meet with our student-athletes individually to set goals for our offseason training. Here are a few examples of formats we have used in past seasons:

Example 1

Describe in detail your goals for spring season in the following areas:

1. Softball skills, strength and conditioning
2. Personal leadership development (What areas of leadership are you already strong in? Where can you stretch yourself to help the team?)
3. Team culture and team chemistry (How do you contribute to the team culture—positively or negatively? What things can you do to contribute to better team chemistry—big or small, on or off the field?)

Example 2

List your outcome goals (long-term goals, specific things about the type of athlete you want to become for spring season).

List your process goals attached to each of your outcome goals (What do you have to do along the way to get the results, or outcome goals, you want?).

It's March 27, and we are set to play our first Ivy League doubleheader:

1. Describe your game-day mental and physical preparation beginning the night before.
2. Describe yourself as an athlete on this day. (How do you channel your nerves? How do you respond to the unexpected? How do you perform?)

These two examples demonstrate an introductory way to help student-athletes foster inner competitiveness by measuring themselves against a goal. Even when no one else is around, student-athletes have tangible, attainable goals to focus their workouts and breed a desire to complete their goals. Notice that the two examples are quite different. The first represents a year when the team needed an in-depth discussion about leadership and team culture. With a small group of upperclassmen, including only two seniors, the rest of the team needed to step up to fill leadership roles and contribute positively to the team culture we set out to create. The second example is much more specific about individual skill development and goals, encouraging team members to take ownership over the work they put in during the offseason. These individual meetings can be adapted to cover the topics relevant to your team that particular year.

Athlete Versus Teammates

Another aspect of building competitiveness within a team is to create situations in which student-athletes are being challenged by their teammates. Some of the biggest jumps I have witnessed in the development and growth of a student-athlete occurred when our coaching staff made intentional, motivating partnerships in non-position-specific training. For example, a sophomore in our program showed great potential and a decent work ethic early in her college career. She was matched up as a lifting partner with a senior who was modest but unapologetic about the effort she put in to every workout. This senior brought a blue-collar attitude to everything she did; she was the first person to arrive and the last to leave, shirt drenched after every session, the epitome of a leader by example. This senior helped unleash an inner fire in our sophomore, and the rest of the team noticed that both were improving weekly in the weight room because of their special partnership. This kind of quiet, encouraging competitiveness between teammates can be realized on any team by being deliberate about the partnerships that coaches create outside positional training.

Competing for positions, on the other hand, creates situations in which student-athletes are grouped with teammates that they often don't have a choice to be grouped with. If you are a pitcher, you're working out with other pitchers. If you are a catcher, you are competing with the other catchers on the team for that starting spot. Friendship and personality similarity or differences often take a backseat in these relationships, and they should. Regardless of the relationship of the athletes in a particular position group, we can find a way to create a positive, productive, and competitive environment in which they can all improve. I believe that to establish competitive position training at practice, the coaching staff must first communicate clear expectations for playing time to the team. If an athlete thinks that she will never have a chance to see the field no matter how hard she works or what improvements she makes, her competitive spirit diminishes and the entire position group suffers. Outlining expectations for each athlete and the steps she needs to take to contribute to the team's success allows the coaching staff to hold her to that standard and allows the athletes in the position group to evaluate themselves in an accurate, realistic way.

Position-Group Collaboration

One of the most beneficial practices we have established on our squad is to have each student-athlete share with others in the position group what she is working on. My own college experience was a good example of this. I was on a pitching staff of incredibly talented pitchers who were very different from me. A senior on our staff threw a heavy, fall-off-the-table drop ball. She was tall, confident, and incredibly intimidating in spite of her inclusive nature as team captain. I was a riseball pitcher, and my dropball was my worst pitch. What better way could I learn than from someone experienced and strong in areas where I was weak to show me what made her successful? The entire year I was too proud and too afraid to ask her for help on a pitch that would have been a great complement to my riseball. After she graduated, I told her how much I could have used her guidance. She responded, "You should have asked!"

Our pitchers share openly with each other what they believe to be the weakest aspects of their pitching repertoire. For certain drills, pitchers are paired based on complementary skill sets, such as a great screwball pitcher with a great curveball pitcher or a flamethrower with someone who mixes speeds and has a strong changeup. They are encouraged to learn from each other, to learn why their partner is strong in a certain pitch, and to try to implement their partner's methods into their own motion. This kind of training does a couple things. First, it allows our pitchers to understand fully their strengths and areas that need improvement. They learn to analyze the motions of the other pitchers on our staff, thus helping them to understand their own mechanics better. The arrangement also breeds camaraderie and healthy competitiveness between pitchers. They make suggestions and talk through the whys and hows of each pitch. It's amazing to see a pitcher come off the mound in season after a rough inning and talk through adjustments she can make with the other pitchers.

Even more special, we had a pitcher on staff who threw hard but lacked an effective changeup. She worked tirelessly in the offseason taking advice from the rest of our pitching staff on how to make her changeup a devastating complement to her speed. During a league game that year, she threw a great changeup for a strikeout. The pitching staff erupted with cheers in the dugout, greeting her with high fives and excitement when she came off the field after the inning. Her win was a win for the whole staff.

Position-Group Competitiveness

Beyond skill development, position groups offer an important opportunity to help student-athletes learn how to deal appropriately with pressure situations. In my experience, a few things happen when teammates in a position group grow accustomed to competing against one another in a practice setting. First, they become desensitized to performing under pressure. We all know student-athletes who are fantastic practice players but struggle to translate their play into game situations. Coaches can implement this mental-training opportunity by creating a consistently competitive environment in practices. This type of athlete needs opportunities outside a game setting to learn how to execute.

Second, they learn to embrace competition rather than fear it. In a softball world where college commitments, sport specialization, and a showcase environment have sucked the life out of young peoples' natural competitive drive, we can reignite some of that fire at practice. One of the best examples that I draw inspiration from is an assistant coach I once worked with. During infield workouts, he started by hitting warm-up reps, in order around the horn. Any time two people were taking reps at one position, our second basemen for instance, he used it as an opportunity to challenge the players there to compete in front of our team. He hit groundball after groundball to the players alternating in at that position, trying to make each round a little bit tougher, testing their range, glove skills, and footwork. The whole team stopped to watch as our second basemen went head to head, making tough play after tough play, never backing down. He hit to them back and forth until someone made a mistake, and then he moved on to hitting in order around the infield again. The best part about it was that he never said a word. You didn't know when it was coming, but when it happened, the team cheered those athletes on, pushing them to compete and challenge one another. We all loved it, secretly hoping that he would single out our position next.

Here are some additional examples of how we promote competition in practices within our position groups.

Pitching Staff Versus Team

Have all pitchers on your staff ready to face a lineup of hitters. They can be ghost batters, athletes on the team tracking, or real hitters, depending on where you are in your season. The pitcher who starts throws the first pitch of the at-bat. The next pitcher throws the next pitch of the at-bat with the 0-1 or 1-0 count. The staff rotates through, throwing only one pitch at a time, completing an inning of batters or a game as a staff. Each pitcher learns to depend on the others to set up the group for success or to pick each other up when someone makes a mistake. This drill is a great camaraderie builder for a pitching staff because they learn how to function as a group rather than as individuals.

Horse

This spin on a popular basketball game can be played with many position groups. We typically use this format with hitters, slappers, and pitchers. The first person up calls her shot. It can be broad (line drive to the left side) or specific (ground ball to the second baseman). If that person succeeds, the player behind her must hit the same shot. Failing at that, she earns a letter. If a player earns enough letters to spell Horse (or the name of your school mascot), she is out of the game. We find this an upbeat and fun game to play that creates a competitive pressure situation for the hitter. It's perfect for slappers who are working on bat control and execution. Finally, we use it with our pitchers one-on-one or as a staff. Again, the focus is on execution in a pressure situation.

Last Person Standing

This challenge can be used for hitting or defense. For hitting, the whole team lines up, and one by one they must execute a line drive to stay in the game. If they do, they're still in and go to the back of the line. If they don't, they're out. A variation is to have players hit as many line drives in a row as they can—whoever hits the most in a row wins. You can do this on defense too. We have an infielder line in the dirt and an outfielder line in the grass. The player must field the ball cleanly and make a good throw to stay in the game. The longer the game goes on, the tougher the rounds get. By the end, everyone should be diving all over the place to stay in the game. We like this from a defensive standpoint because it breeds fearlessness. If you play not to lose, chances are you will make a mistake. We encourage our athletes to focus on the process of winning rather than the outcome. If they trust their training and mechanics, they'll be successful in this game.

Partner Motivation

Tapping into thoughtful pairings of athletes, one of the most interesting discussions you can have with your team is learning who on the team motivates them. Go around the whole group to let each team member identify which of her teammates motivates her at practice and why. Taking this to the next level, you can pair athletes together or have them pair themselves with teammates who motivate them. Then take them through a hitting circuit. You can do this on a normal reps day, just allowing the athletes to interact and challenge each other. You can also assign point values to stations, allowing them to compete at each station with someone who inspires them to get better.

When you begin to tackle establishing a competitive environment within position groups on your team, two important things are to (1) institute routines with an athlete's approach and (2) be creative with practice structure. Setting expectations for how that position group will interact and how they will practice is essential for promoting competitiveness. The kind of routines you implement within a position group greatly enhances their ability to compete with each other and eventually with an opponent. If the coaching staff sets the expectation that position groups will challenge each other every day, they become accustomed to training in a consistently competitive environment, which promotes the growth of all members of that position group. Being creative in the structure of these practices allows your players to be exposed to different kinds of challenges that may come up in a game setting. Taking it a step further, regulating the amount of pressure the team is experiencing at practice can help team members develop competitiveness whatever the environment is around them.

Team Versus Practice

To transfer competition at practice into game situations, the team needs to develop a sense of group competitiveness as well. We like to call this team versus practice. Practice is structured in a way that allows the group to compete toward a goal. This type of practice structure allows all team members to pull in one direction as a group rather than compete with their teammates. Teams have a distinct opportunity to gel competitively as a group when they all are working toward a goal. We set the stage for these practices by announcing team goals at the beginning of practice before warm-ups so that they can begin to prepare mentally for what is in store. If two or three goals are set for a practice, each of them has a process-driven approach that is reinforced by our coaching staff before that segment of practice begins.

For example, if we are working through a hitting circuit and focusing on laying off changeups, the outcome goal is to have no swings at changeups during batting practice. The team is challenged to focus on what the process will be to achieve that goal (i.e., separate stride foot and hands firing). When each athlete cycles through batting practice successfully without swinging at a changeup, she is praised for staying focused on the process and doing her part in working toward the team's goal. If we achieve the team goal, we talk about why we got there—that it took all 20 team members to trust in the process and focus on getting their part of the job done. If we don't meet the goal, the next step is to identify why we fell short and what we would do differently if the practice were repeated. In this setting, athletes get used to the idea of being part of a whole and gain a better understanding of their contributions toward a team goal. It also allows the team to generate a sense of competitiveness as a unit.

For a team to grab on to a competitive practice environment, they need to participate fully in creating it. If athletes have a sense of ownership over practices, they're more likely to respond positively to challenges. A simple way of allowing the team members to exhibit ownership over competitions in practice is to allow them to establish the goals that the team must meet. You have a few opportunities to do this on a weekly, if not daily, basis. The first is during team defense. The team gets to determine how many clean outs they can make in seven innings—no errors, physical or mental. When you try this the first time at practice, chances are that the team will low-ball themselves to ensure that they achieve the goal. With some encouragement and after some success, the team will get to the point where they want to see how far they can go. They'll start craving 21 clean outs instead of settling for 17 in a full seven innings of defense. From an offensive standpoint, something as simple as setting a goal for how many line drives they can hit consecutively as a team, going person by person, like an at-bat, can be hugely beneficial. Again, allowing the team to take ownership over the level of competitiveness they want to create for themselves gets buy in. Eventually, with some consistency and encouragement, you'll see results.

Team Versus the Other Guys

Finally, we get to the game, the competitive setting that matters most! Or does it? Of course, there are athletes on every team who come alive when the first pitch is thrown. Called gamers, or, as Dick Vitale, sportscaster and former collegiate and professional coach, would say, "prime-time players" or "PTPers," these athletes have almost a sixth sense for turning it on and performing when they can taste real competition. These outliers can be a real catalyst for a team in games. For the athletes on a team who don't have this innate quality, some development and training is needed to get them to the point where they are comfortable in game situations, especially in a sport where failure happens often.

The game environment is secondary to and a result of the practice environment when it comes to competitiveness. It all starts with how a team trains. If a hitter has trained not to swing at changeups in the cage at practice, she is more likely to be successful in a game situation facing a pitcher who has a good changeup. Every pitch, then, is a chance to compete. A curveball that catches the corner of the strike zone is a win for the pitcher. A cleanly fielded ground ball and strong throw from the shortstop is a win for the shortstop and for the defense. What is unique about softball is that we can deeply influence the result of the game with just one pitch. That circumstance can be overwhelming to a pitcher who fears throwing a ball down the middle or to an infielder who doesn't want the ball hit to her when a runner is on third. But if these athletes have trained for these situations, they embrace the opportunity to win rather than indulge in worry about potential failure.

The same process-based approach used in practice can be used in games in meaningful ways. Many things happen through the course of the game that you can't control: weather, the umpires, the opponent, parents, and so on. What you can control is your mind-set and your process. A great way to trigger the same process-focused team that you train in practice is to set goals before the game and allow the team to participate in creating those goals. Make sure that most are process-based goals controllable by the team. Posting these goals in the dugout can be compelling for the team. You can post them on a whiteboard or clipboard, or put each athlete in charge of holding a card with the goal on it—to be ripped up in celebration if the goal is achieved. Here is a list of goals you can use:

- Run on every pitched ball in the dirt.
- Hitters attack the first strike.
- Execute all routine plays on defense.
- Pitchers throw 70 percent first-pitch strikes.
- Move three runners over with the short game.
- All team members communicate after every pitch.

In all these examples, athletes have a controllable focus that keeps them grounded in things they already know from practice.

Sometimes, however, getting caught up in what is a success and what is a failure can derail us from achieving our goals. One of the best examples of how to handle this is my assistant coach's approach and response to at-bats in games. Many times an athlete comes off the field after an at-bat disappointed with a groundout or, worse, frustrated with a line drive that was caught. In each situation, the assistant talks that athlete through what went well in her swing. If the groundout was working on her barrel taking a more direct path to the ball and she just got on top of the pitch, that is a positive takeaway from the at-bat that demonstrates progress. If the athlete who hit a line drive comes off disappointed with not getting a base hit, the assistant coach reminds her that she did her job, put a good swing on the right pitch, and will soon have a bloop single fall in. What my assistant coach does well is to refocus our athletes on the process. In turn, athletes learn to appreciate the small victories and learn from their mistakes rather than wallow in them.

Last One Syndrome

Our practice environment must not protect our athletes from failure. Instead, our athletes should experience failure often, and then be coached on how to deal with it, individually and as a team. One of the most interesting anomalies of our sport is last one syndrome. When throwing batting practice, whether working at a camp or training my own athletes, as soon as I say, "Last one," something remarkable happens to the hitter. She tenses, her bat speed decreases, and she mishits her last ball. With a short spurt of disappointment, she rebounds and says, "Can I have another one?" This moment is exceptionally teachable. The last one in a round of batting practice is a simplified version of being in an at-bat. It's a pressure situation whether or not the athletes recognize it, and it offers you a great opportunity to show them how to deal with it. When our athletes experienced this, we talked through why they weren't successful hitting the last pitch of a round. They had to recognize that they had a physical response to the cue "last one," and they needed to learn how to combat that tension and refocus on the process of taking a good swing. Then, regardless of the result of the last ball, they leave the cage. They're then asked to evaluate what was good about their swing, what mistake they made if they didn't get the result they wanted, and what they would do differently next time.

The Positivity Myth

Along a similar vein, a common thought is that athletes should always finish on something positive. Certainly, we all have those rough days at practice when everything is a grind and nothing seems to be going right. Those are the days to finish on something positive. For the other days, this positivity mantra can be destructive for athletes who don't know how to fail and recover from failure. On many days our players don't finish on something positive. On some days they finish on something ugly, unathletic, or poorly executed. We make them walk away from the day and close practice. They're welcome to do a couple things if their failure gets to them: (1) get on a tee or (2) talk it out. Tee work or any kind of reps they can get by themselves develops their ability to control the controllable—their preparation. They can take extra reps and make a correction on a tee, but have to wait until the next day to get back in the batter's box. Having the ability to talk things out with a teammate or coach about why the day was a struggle and why they're frustrated can be cathartic and allows them the opportunity to evaluate some of the emotions they are likely experiencing in games as well. In a game of failure, it's easy to develop a play-not-to-lose mentality.

Instead, you want athletes to play fearlessly. If failure happens, and it will, you need to teach them how to handle it in a healthy and appropriate way that motivates them to be better next time.

Conditioning Competitiveness

To get a team to be at the height of motivation and excitement for competition, the players have to practice it. When athletes are consistently training in a competitive practice setting, experiencing pressure situations, failures, and emotional highs and lows, they become desensitized to them. Conditioning athletes to let go of those potential barriers to optimal performance leaves something beautiful on the field—raw competitiveness. No other factor is more important than the will to compete. Coaches should strive to create this special feeling for the athletes on their team.

Our coaching staff gets pumped for competition. We as coaches have to set the example for why and how competition makes us a better team by embracing it. When a player at practice steps up to make a great play in a pressure situation, we take time to celebrate her effort and fearlessness. We sometimes forget how much influence the coaching staff has on our student-athletes' approach to the game. Our assumption is that competitiveness is inherent and cannot be developed. The fun of athletics is all about competition—mastery of a skill (competition with self), execution under pressure, winning the play, and winning the game.

In seeking to develop a competitive environment in a team, take the approach that how you do anything is how you do everything. The comfort level that athletes have in pressure situations on a ball field is a direct reflection of the environment that they train in every day. Athletes respond to consistency. If the environment you establish in agility training, individual workouts, team workouts, and practices is consistently competitive, chances are your team will be successful on game days. For a team to embrace competition within themselves, with their teammates, and on game day, they must practice it.

Chapter 6

Motivating Players in Practices

Dot Richardson, MD

To reach the goal of obtaining not only perfect practices but also perfect games, coaches must understand what motivation is and make it a priority to teach and instill it within their athletes.

A coach is a teacher and mentor. A coach teaches the fundamentals and strategies of the game and, more important, is a huge influence in the life of an athlete. In fact, a coach will influence the lives of more people in one year than most people will in a lifetime. Getting your athletes to believe in themselves and their talents so that they are internally motivated is the ultimate goal, the secret to success. When your athletes have true motivation for the game and other aspects of their lives, they will come closer to reaching their full potential. If you make a commitment to work toward influencing your players to become more self-driven, self-confident, and self-assured, you will experience success that reaches way beyond the playing field.

Striving for perfection is the process by which we get closer to perfect performance in practice and games. Coaches need to understand this process and be true motivators—people who inspire, think of others before themselves, and act in ways that show they care. These coaches know that their role is to serve and influence the lives of others in positive ways. They have a commitment to make a difference in the lives of players and know that doing so is a privilege.

Coaches who motivate recognize that actions speak louder than words. They also realize that the sport is more than a game, that life lessons can be learned, and that they need to point them out to their players. The game can build character, confidence, and self-esteem if a coach leads the way. Everything a coach does influences these young athletes in every aspect of their lives, way beyond the playing field. The following comes from my collegiate coaching staff to our players:

> As your coaching staff, we recognize that we have been chosen by God to be a part of your life and at this time in your lives. We are humbled and honored for this opportunity and responsibility. We are committed to serve you. We take it seriously. We pray that you feel the same, honored to be a part of the University and the softball team and serious about being committed to excellence both on and off the field! Together, we are stronger. We will be given each day the opportunities to live our dreams. . . . Let's prepare ourselves through hard work, teamwork, belief, fight, and faith! The following are our goals for you:
>
> - To develop an inner motivation and desire to make a positive contribution and impact in the people and world around you
> - To strive for excellence in everything you say and do
> - To take responsibility for your actions and have a quest for your actions to only have positive impact in games, practices, and socially
> - To achieve the greatness you are meant to experience
> - To remove all doubt and let your talents be free to express themselves as you display that joy both on and off the field

What coach are you committed to be? Is it all about the Xs and Os? Or is it about much more? Ask yourself, "Why do I coach?" and "What influence do I want to have in the lives of those around me?" Your answers to these questions will guide the leadership role you will play and the importance you will place on understanding motivation.

True Motivation

So what motivates you to be a coach? Do you coach because it gives you some identity? Or because it gives you a position of authority and power? Is it to satisfy your want for competition so that you can boast about your records or accomplishments? Or is it because you want to affect the lives of your players in positive ways? Or because you want to help others reach their full potential? A coach can motivate others to excel or to repel. In the quest for perfect practices leading to perfect game performances, it has to be about your players, not you. The best way to motivate others is to put others' needs before yours. It is not about your wants, but about theirs. It takes a servant's heart. When players know that you want the best for each of them, you have built a foundation of trust and respect. If you are motivated to help your athletes be the best they can be in every aspect of their lives, your drive for them will eventually result in each of your athletes developing that same drive and passion for herself. This process is the ultimate transformation to true motivation, the development of an inner drive to be the best one can be no matter what the circumstances. And it begins with you, the coach. When you have committed yourself to becoming a motivational coach, you are getting closer to reaching the goal of being a success.

True motivation must come from within. Unfortunately, many players lack self-motivation because they do not realize that they have the power and control within themselves to possess it. Each of us has amazing gifts and opportunities. We should embrace every chance we have to demonstrate those talents.

A Life Coach

Many players lack self-confidence and look to others to find happiness and feelings of self-worth, accomplishment, or even well-being. In fact, people want to be loved so much that they are willing to do whatever it takes to feel loved, to be accepted, or to fit in. Unfortunately, they will do whatever it takes to be accepted, even when they are uncomfortable and know that their actions are wrong. Are you a coach who cares about your players beyond the field? Are you willing to go beyond the instruction of the fundamentals of the game to teach life lessons of empowerment and worth to your players so that they can resist false thoughts or real temptations? Players should recognize that no one, not even the game, defines who they are because each of them is special and valued.

So how do you know what motivates your players? A quick way to find out is to have them fill out a questionnaire answering specific questions such as these: Why do you play the sport? What do you like about the game? What are some of your athletic goals? What are some of your personal goals? What do you like to do in your off time? How do you see your life in 10 years? Answers to these self-awareness questions will let you know a little more about your players and their motivations. You will find out whether they are playing to be with their friends, to have fun, to be on a team, or to compete because of love for the game. By doing this simple exercise, you will be amazed to see how much your players will begin to realize that you care about them not only as players but also as people. And when they know that you care, they will care about what you have to say.

Attitude and Effort

Most people don't realize how much power they have to motivate themselves. For example, people can control two things in their life and on the field— their attitude and their effort. Athletes can decide whether they are going to have a positive outlook or not. The drive for a perfect practice begins with an athlete having a positive attitude to achieve perfection. An athlete may realize that perfection is rarely obtained, but simply pursuing perfection as an inner motivation helps the person come closer to reaching her full potential. Athletes have the choice to give everything they have in an effort to pursue perfection. They can decide to give everything they have, nothing at all, or anything in between. Your athletes need to learn that a positive attitude with a commitment to excel in effort will help them come closer to reaching their full potential and closer to performance perfection in practices and games.

Frustrations

Coaches know that three things lead to frustration; two of them are that they know their athletes can control their attitude and effort, yet their players elect to have a poor attitude and give little effort. The third is seeing the potential of an athlete who doesn't believe she has it or doesn't try to achieve it. Instead, the athlete is comfortable with settling. One of the most important motivational roles of coaches is to instill in their athletes self-confidence—a belief in themselves and their abilities. An athlete can do this when she knows that someone believes in her; as a coach, you can be influential in this process. In time, with supportive coaching, an athlete will start to believe in herself more and more. As each athlete on a team gains more self-confidence, more confidence develops within the team and for the team. Ultimately, to achieve the best performances in practices and games, each athlete needs to commit to pursuing excellence and refusing to be the weakest link of the team. This self-driven and self-inspired pursuit of excellence grows stronger as an athlete experiences more success on the field.

A Teacher, a Mentor

Another way to instill motivation in your players and build their self-confidence is to focus on teaching the fundamentals of the game. When you make this commitment to your players, whether starters or nonstarters, they begin to believe that you care about how they do and that you want the best for them. Your players will buy into your coaching style and be more receptive to learning from you, especially when they see that your teaching helps them and their teammates perform better. If your athletes know that you want the best for each of them, not some of them but all of them, then you are on your way to getting closer to achieving perfect performances.

As a coach, you need to emphasize to your athletes the importance of making a commitment to learn, understand, and execute the fundamentals of the sport. Construct your practice plan to include drills, classroom settings, and position plays that enforce proper mechanics. The quest toward mastering these fundamentals brings an athlete closer to reaching her full potential. A few secrets to help your athletes master the skills of the game are to enforce how each movement feels to the player, to receive their input, and to provide immediate feedback verbally and with video analysis if possible.

Also, teach the players how to visualize their performance. If athletes can visualize their skills and plays in games, they will learn quicker and perform better. As an athlete begins to execute the fundamentals consistently, her performance improves and she experiences more success. She gains greater confidence and more motivation to succeed again. This pursuit of mastering and consistently executing the basic skills causes your players to improve.

Whatever level you reach in the sport, the team that best executes the fundamentals of the game is usually the team that wins. So invest in understanding and teaching the fundamentals. As you teach, do so with the understanding that learning occurs at different stages and through different means. You have to identify the skill level of each of your players and the most effective ways to teach each of them. Familiarize yourself with all the options available to you and look at them as amazing opportunities. One of the basic teaching principles is that people must be able to do a movement first without an object before they do it with an object, like a ball or bat. Also, athletes must be able to perform a skill correctly at a slow speed before they advance to doing it at full speed. Take your time to teach properly. Don't be in a rush; your time will be well spent in doing it right no matter how long it takes.

Implement practice drills that start with the basics and then progress to the more advanced aspects. Move from slow to faster speeds and from less pressure to more. Begin with simple freeze drills to emphasize the proper mechanics. Then advance to game speed and conditions. Commit to always emphasizing the proper execution of fundamentals. Don't settle for almost right. Never say to yourself, "She'll never get it. I give up." Stay committed and motivated to do what it takes to take your athletes to the next level and beyond.

Practice Like a Game

The next level in building more motivation to perfect practice and game performance is teaching your athletes the offensive and defensive strategies of the game. To accomplish this goal, use practices and classroom settings to produce game-like situations. At practice, do walk-throughs for every possible scenario and then advance to more game-like situations, including mock games and scrimmages. As the coach, you should continue to emphasize the execution of proper mechanics and positioning through every play. In the classroom, use a whiteboard and video analysis of practice and game footage to open conversations. Throughout this progression of learning, more happens than just better physical performance during games. Athletes become more focused, mentally stronger, and more confident.

If you commit to developing motivated players and performances, the changes will quickly become evident. Players become more confident in their decision making. They trust their instincts and play with less thinking and more reaction. They appear to have less fear or doubt. At practices and in games, they are less distracted and more determined. They perform better and more consistently. They handle their mistakes more easily and make fewer of them. They become more self-driven, self-assured, and self-motivated. The by-product is that both players and coaches are more excited to play in games and more eager to compete.

When you design practices, keep in mind that the ultimate goal is to help each of your athletes achieve self-motivation. The structure of your practices can inspire this development. We spoke earlier about developing strong fundamentals through practice plans. When your players become consistent in executing the fundamentals, advance your practices to challenge them more, both mentally and physically. Put your athletes in an environment that tests their skills, their mind-set, and their physical ability. With challenging practices, athletes can quickly increase their defensive range and improve their offensive consistency and strength, as well as develop mental awareness, alertness, and toughness. By pushing their limits and moving out of their comfort zone, players may be astonished that they can make plays they didn't think were possible. Athletes may never know how great they can be unless they have a coach preparing them for success in every aspect of the game.

Practice Design

Another way to keep athletes motivated during practices is to make sure that the sessions are organized, creative, moving, and energized. Always have a purpose and organize each practice accordingly. All your athletes should be involved; no one should be bored or standing around. Variety in practices will keep players interested and motivated. Advancing practices to simulate games will elevate their preparation for competition. They will become more motivated to compete because they are more confident in what they can do. To prepare for games further, consider scouting your opponents and exposing your players to the upcoming challenges. Continue to advance to more challenging drills and situational plays as your athletes advance in skill and motivation. Again, to reiterate, never lose sight of reinforcing the execution of the proper fundamentals of the game, even in competition. As a coach, when you get to the point where you can see your team play with self-confidence and self-motivation and all you need to do is offer an occasional comment on fundamentals or clarify a game situation, then you know you are a successful coach, whatever the score of the game is.

An athlete who is motivated to strive for perfect performances has the ability to remove all doubts and distractions. She can focus on whatever task is at hand. She lives in the moment, and is one with the ball at both practices and games. This athlete looks at competition as a celebration to challenge herself and show her gifts. She is motivated to practice as if practice were a game. She is driven by a desire to master the fundamentals. She prepares

Ingredients for Motivating Players in Practice

The following are the ingredients for motivating practice perfect softball:

- Emphasize the fundamentals of the game.
- Emphasize the execution of each of those fundamentals.
- Emphasize the feeling of the game, not just going through the motions to perform in the game.
- Design the practice to be like a game by putting the players in game-like situations.
- Design the practice with the intensity of a game.
- Design the practice with energy and excitement.
- Speed up the practice but teach the athletes how to stay focused and be in the moment by slowing down the game.
- Prepare your athletes for competition. Scouting and game preparation will help the athletes experience what the game can present. Then, on game day, they are familiar with what can happen and their performance seems routine.
- Prepare your practices with common routines in preparation for practices and games.
- Teach the players that putting on their cleats, before practice or a game, is the trigger for them to clear their minds and commit to the task at hand, which is performing during practice or the game.
- Know what motivates the players so that you can help them be motivated to play.
- Know what each player's strengths and weaknesses are and work to strengthen them both.
- Teach mental training in practice so that it is eventually translated into competitive performances.
- Put each player in game situations repeatedly. Learned behavior is enhanced in competition as the athlete begins to feel more confident in her abilities.
- Teach and inspire so that each of your athletes feels prepared.
- Correct fundamental flaws so that lack of fundamental strengths doesn't cause performance failure.
- Teach so that each athlete feels as if she can perform the skills of the game by second nature—without thought, by reaction only.
- Teach the athletes how to clear their minds of any distractions and be truly in the moment.
- Encourage the athletes to be aggressive, to trust their skills, and to do what they have been taught and prepared to do.
- Keep practices organized and purposeful.

(continued)

Ingredients for Motivating Players in Practice *(continued)*

- Prepare practices with the goal of reinforcing the fundamentals of the game. Put those fundamentals through game situations and competitive strategies so that everything become instinctive and familiar.

- Teach the players to stay true to themselves by trusting their skills, their talent, and their preparation. Those who fail to prepare, prepare to fail, so the secret is to prepare.

- Teach the athletes that what they can control is what they should work to master. The outcome is uncontrollable.

- The perfect practice occurs when players give everything they have physically, mentally, and emotionally.

- Teach the athletes that when they fail or fall short of their goals, they are not failures.

- Teach the athletes that when they succeed, they are not better than anyone else.

- Teach your athletes that practice makes permanent.

- Teach your athletes the true meaning of success. Success is not being at least one run ahead of the other team; true success is giving everything you have to be the best you can be no matter what the circumstances. A true champion never makes excuses; instead, she gives it everything she has each moment she can give it in every situation she experiences.

- Teach your athletes never to focus on winning or losing but instead to execute the fundamentals of the game. With proper teaching and individual motivation to excel, winning will take care of itself.

- Teach your athletes to remove all doubt and fear.

- The goal of a perfect practice is to build confidence through execution that is brought into the game.

- The ultimate motivation results in becoming one with the ball. Nothing else exists except what actually exists at that point in practice or the game.

- Teach the players that giving all they have on the field, both in practice and in games, is perfect, whatever the outcome.

herself physically, mentally, and spiritually. She has true motivation, that internal drive to be the best she can be in everything she does. Nobody can take away her passion for the game and competition.

Motivation is a key factor in reaching one's full potential. People need to search within themselves to learn what truly motivates them. When people find the why to their drive, they can formulate goals and structure to help them achieve what they set out to accomplish. Is it to be the best that they can be? Is it to make a difference in the lives of others along the way? Remember, if you lead a team, your players want to know that you care about them and believe in them. True leaders recognize how special their players are and treat them that way. God has made each of us unique and gifted for a reason, and these differences are what can make a team amazing. We all have the opportunity to show these gifts in our sport, and we should never take that opening for granted.

Imagine that you are the coach who creates a strong, confident, exceptional athlete who recognizes her gifts and opportunities and is now ready to seize those opportunities to be the best she can be in everything she does. And it all started by your showing her, through action and example, that you believed in her. You told her how special she is, strengthened her strengths and weaknesses, encouraged her to be who she was born to be. Because of your belief in her, she now believes more in herself. The result is a more prepared, instinctive, and motivated athlete who emerges in competition. And that is perfect.

Chapter 7

Organizing Effective Batting Practices

Ken Eriksen

Although every coach laments, "There is just not enough time in the day to accomplish what we need to get done," she or he needs to figure out how to maximize the time allotment and be effective, efficient, and economical.

Batting practice (BP) or hitting practice (HP) that is part of the daily overall practice plan has to be slotted in where it makes the most sense given the objectives of the day. If you are going to scrimmage, then putting BP in the beginning of practice may be wise. If the objectives are defense and the intensity is going to be at maximum effort, putting BP at the end may be more beneficial. Either way, the head coach or staff has to figure out what best fits that day's objectives.

When putting your overall practice plan together (whether for the week, the month, or longer), you need to have a plan for your hitting. Teaching hitting and practicing hitting are two different things. The teaching should be done in small-group settings or on an individual basis. The practice parts of hitting are numerous in nature. Many approaches are viable. The number of drills is enormous, and so is the number of gimmicks.

But if you want to use your team's time efficiently, you should be using applicable drills that can help translate your practicing of skills into real game results. With that in mind, every coach asks whether to incorporate the pitching staff in hitting practice. I'll address that important question later.

Just as important as the details of your players' ability to help your team win are the abilities among your coaches to move hitting practice along and make it effective. If you are using multiple rotations during your practice, each section must be on the same page with the approach to the objectives.

Set Reasonable Goals

What are the objectives of your hitting practice? Objectives are likely to change through the course of a season. In the beginning of your practice season (as you prepare for the upcoming season), hitting practice should probably be geared toward timing and eye tracking. As the weeks progress, you are probably progressing toward bat control approaches and repetitive sequencing. As the hitters become more comfortable and the timing factors all look good, you likely go to maintenance mode. Sound easy? It's not. As your athletes become older and stronger, they are constantly going through an evolutionary process in their hitting. So how do you, as a coach, remain consistent in your teaching and approach to practice? How do you incorporate repetition without allowing it to become stale? At what point are rest and recovery implemented? Last and most important is leadership. Are you clear and concise in your teaching?

Timing Is Everything

We are trying to fit into slots everything that we want to get across to our students. The main problem is that we are limited by several factors:

- Class schedules
- Our family schedules
- Facility schedules
- Unaccounted daily inhibitors

So how do we structure our practice plans for hitting as we progress through our seasons? As stated earlier, you must (knowing the level of your team) have a plan that is realistic in its approach to preparing for the season. Some teams may work more on bunting. Some may focus on timing, and others may work on strategic approaches (bat control plays or swinging for the fences). For this chapter I start at base level and then let you as the coach decide whether to increase the speed of your approach or slow it down. With only a month to prepare for our season, the following plan can be broken down into four weeks of training.

Week 1

One hour and 15 minutes (75 minutes) of batting practice with five rotations that include (but are not limited to)

- a live hitting section (five rounds of three),
- a center toss drill section (seven rounds of three),
- a tee work drill section (four rounds of five),
- a live defensive section, and
- a baserunning section (starting at first base on day 1 and moving to a different base each day after explaining the rules for each base).

You need to incorporate as much as you can during your hitting practice. The defensive section is not just a shag section. We have our defensive players approach each pitch as they are in their positions. Over time we have had great success with getting better reads on the ball during games. We use the same philosophy with baserunning. Early in the season we win games with our defense, pitching, and baserunning. The bats eventually warm up if they are cool early on.

As important as it is to go through week 1, you should assess with your coaches where you are. I don't recommend progressing faster than your team is capable.

Week 2

One hour and 15 minutes (75 minutes) of batting practice with five rotations that include (but are not limited to)

- a live hitting section (after each round, run out the last one live and let the defense play that ball live with a runner);

   round 1—two sacrifice bunts, three opposite-field ground balls;

   round 2—three hit aways;

   round 3—three hit aways;

   round 4—three hit away, bunt for a hit;

   round 5—three hit aways, squeeze;

- a center toss drill section (three rounds of seven balls total with only five being strikes);
- a tee work drill section (four rounds of five);
- a live defensive section; and
- because the baserunning is done from the plate this week, another defensive live section.

As we continue to progress toward week 3, the coaching staff continues to teach skills in the batting cages. At the same time, they limit the talk when the players are hitting live. Players must have a clear mind to be able to figure out their approach. As tough as it is for teachers not to instruct on every pitch, players need to develop on their own. Coaches and players can talk after the rounds, but they should avoid chatter during the rounds.

Weeks 3 and 4

These two weeks depend on how well your team is adapting to your teaching. Are they good with their bunts? Are they good with bat control? If they are, then you have to decide how to implement certain things during your live rounds, such as hit and runs (with the baserunners), count hitting (0-0, 2-0, 3-1, with 2 strikes), and moving runners with no outs.

One hour and 15 minutes (75 minutes) of batting practice with five rotations that include (but are not limited to)

- a live hitting section (after each round, run out the last one live and let the defense play that ball live with a runner),

    round 1—two sacrifice bunts, three opposite-field ground balls;

    round 2—three hit aways;

    round 3—three sacrifice flys, squeeze;

    round 4—three count hits (2-0, 3-2, 1-2);

    round 5—batter's choice;

- a center toss drill section (three rounds of seven balls total with only five being strikes);
- a tee work drill section (four rounds of five);
- a live defensive section; and
- because the baserunning is done from the plate this week, another defensive live section.

Remember that this basic four-week preseason batting practice plan is efficient because we incorporate live game-speed defense and live game-speed baserunning.

Practice Plans

To make this work, you need to have facilities that are close to each other. If you don't have a batting cage available, you may have to add a section that is strictly a shag section for the center toss and tee ball work. Use your creativity, another essential part of coaching! Nets and screens can help make your practices more efficient.

To help make this approach more visual to you, I am including a few practice plans from each week leading up to a season (see tables 7.1-7.3). A useful feature of these plans is that each section can be transitioned out for another area of training at any time.

Table 7.1   Practice Example Day 1, Week 1

2:00–2:15 p.m.	Dynamic physical stretching of the muscle groups	
2:15–2:25 p.m.	Throwing program	
2:25–2:55 p.m.	Position skill work	Defense live, live full outs from your position
2:55–3:20 p.m.	Team defense I	Batting area I, tee work, four rounds of five
3:20–3:40 p.m.	Team defense II	Batting area II, center toss, seven rounds of three
3:45–5:00 p.m.	Hitting practice	Live hitting, five rounds of three

Baserunning starts at first base and moves to the next base depending on how the ball is hit |

As we begin to progress over the weeks, we like to advance our hitting and defensive work. Table 7.2 is a day when you don't need to go over a lot of defensive or offensive strategies:

Table 7.2   Practice Example Day 3, Week 3

2:00–2:15 p.m.	Dynamic physical stretching of the muscle groups
2:15–2:25 p.m.	Throwing program
2:25–2:55 p.m.	Position skill work for outfielders and catchers, tee and center toss work for infielders
2:55–3:25 p.m.	Position skill work for infielders, tee and center toss work for outfielders, bullpen work for pitchers and catchers
3:25–5 p.m.	Hitting practice, baserunning

Planning is crucial to achieving team hitting success. The plans should be adaptable to ensure that maximum time is spent on the deficient areas of your team's hitting in preparing them for the upcoming season.

Teaching Versus Hitting

At times team hitting practice will not be enough. Your athletes want personal attention, and this is the best time to learn about them. I have been around the game long enough to realize that several approaches to hitting can be successful, not just one. The one-on-one sessions with your hitters are beneficial for attending to details. Yes, these sessions are time consuming. Yes, you will be working more hours as a coach-teacher. You need to recognize that spending quality time with each hitter can only make your hitters better. You will become a better teacher by bonding a little more with your hitters. Use this time to work on specific items that can be ingrained for long-term success. Remember to be consistent in your approach and acknowledge each hitter's unique personality. Depending on the age of your players, you will see marked improvements at some point. The extra benefit to this personal time is that your language cues will help the team hitting rotations during practice go smoother.

When all your hitters are working together in practice, less is better as far as instruction goes. Team practice should run smoothly. Avoid the pitfall of overcoaching in group settings. At some point, hitters are going to have to go to the plate by themselves. This is the time to let them hit.

Regarding the practice schedules shown earlier, I think that you need to be creative in your planning. Look ahead and figure out when it will be a good time to incorporate live hitting off a pitcher on your staff. These sessions will help both your hitters and your pitchers prepare for the season. At the college level we incorporate live hitting in the second week of a four-week preparation season. For your level it may be later. Table 7.3 is an example of either scrimmage days or live offensive sections with live pitching.

Table 7.3   Practice Example Day 3, Week 2

2:00–2:15 p.m.	Dynamic physical stretching of the muscle groups	
2:15–2:25 p.m.	Throwing program	
2:25–2:55 p.m.	Position skill work	Defense live II, live full outs from your position
2:55–4 p.m.	Hitting practice	

Using Your Coaching Staff

As the head coach or as the person in charge of hitting, you owe it to your team to put the best possible personnel in the lineup to help your team win. The same goes for hitting practice. The difference this time is that your team personnel are your coaching staff. Each member must believe that her or his contribution is essential to the overall good. Whether the staff member is handling fungo ground balls, teaching baserunning, throwing live batting practice, being the center toss person, or just watching mechanics, you need to explain how you want this part of practice to run. Practicing practice (for our coaching staff and players) is what we do early in the year. This way, when we get into the third day of our preseason, the machine is running smoothly.

Having someone who can throw fastpitch softball hitting practice is helpful. Because hitting is timing, a machine does not enhance the natural sequencing of the timing aspect of hitting. I am not going to go into the sequence itself (words you have heard before—loading, landing, toe touch, heel plant, and so on) because this chapter is not about all of that and because I believe that most of this is irrelevant when it comes to getting the barrel to the ball naturally. Getting back to the discussion of live pitching, I recommend not using your pitchers to throw strictly batting practice. When they throw against your hitters, it is not batting practice; it is competitive practice. The pitchers are trying to get the hitters out, and the hitters are trying to hit the ball hard somewhere. For working on hitting, a coach should throw and pinpoint locations to work on. Your pitchers should pitch competitive hitting practice and focus on defense as well as pitching. A number of pitchers have been hit by comebackers because they have been focused on pitching batting practice. When pitchers are throwing their intention should be to get the hitter out and to work on their pitches in a game-like situation. This is also a good time to let the catcher call the pitches even if a coach calls them during a game.

Keeping Practice Fun

In softball (as in baseball), monotonous, repetitive teaching is what we do. The aspect of fun is incorporated in the successes that each player is achieving. I am not saying that we can't have a fun approach to teaching, but we are seriously teaching repetitive skill work as we go through the season. The plays (hit and runs, sacrifice bunts, squeezes, slap and runs, bunts for a hit, and so on) are different, but the process of getting the bat to the ball doesn't vary much. So with that in mind, you again need to plan a progression of objectives to accomplish through the process. Whether you are working on hitting the ball to the opposite field, hitting more ground balls, whatever—you need to assess your team's performance and talk to your players about accomplishing the tasks together.

As mentioned earlier, the fun part comes in accomplishing the objectives. At the same time we are dealing with young people. So how can you as a creative coach incorporate fun into your batting practice? The following suggestions can help.

Music

Listening to music during batting practice and even dancing between tasks is not a sign of a lack of focus among your athletes. The thought process of lack of focus probably originated from coaches who never played beyond high school. An example of this is the pregame music played at major league baseball games and college games (baseball and softball). Let your players create the playlist and you will find that they are a little more energized during batting practice. It will help them eliminate the distractions of game day and focus on the task at hand. Plus, you may even find that you like the music of the younger generation.

Competitive Games

In baserunning decision making and scoring on bunts, how successful were your players? Establishing teams to go through the entire BP can enhance competitiveness. Competitive games with consequences can help your team develop intensity. A reward system helps them understand that success creates a positive outcome while the vice versa is also true. Some examples of rewards will be given in the next section. These games and challenges also make practice more fun as players' cheer for each other. Develop a point system for each game and each task you want to emphasize.

Rewards

Whether you reward your players by giving them extra swings or allowing the winners to do something special, offering an incentive heightens competition.

I recognize that not everyone reading this book and this chapter has the resources or the personnel that we have on our teams in college or the national team programs. But the beautiful part of coaching is learning how to be creative within your system to be effective, efficient, and successful with your team. Good luck!

Chapter 8

Organizing Effective Fielding Practices

Celeste Knierim

A lot of preparation goes into having effective fielding practices. It all starts with teaching and practicing the fundamental skills needed to be successful playing the game of softball. The organizational skills of the coaching staff are extremely important in planning what to teach during the season.

Establishing Fundamentals

Before a team can prosper and learn from their practices, they must first establish some fundamental skills. All the practices and games on a team's schedule may not produce victories unless proper mechanics and fundamentals are taught in the beginning. If they are not, the players will practice the same mistakes and bad habits over and over every day. Practicing those mistakes will not improve the skill level of the player or the team.

A checklist of some of the important fundamental skills and techniques needed for improvement and success on the field consists of the following:

1. Toes Slightly Turned In

Something as simple as teaching every player to turn her toes in slightly will make her quicker on defense. When the toes are pointing outward, the player is on her heels, which slows her reaction to the ball. She first has to start the motion to get on her toes before she can react to the ball. Players who have their toes pointed slightly inward can do that quicker. Those players will have a better reaction time because their weight is already forward, which cuts out a step in reacting to the ball.

For example, look at the feet of the third and first basemen of the team that you are playing. If they are on their heels, they may be more susceptible to a bunt or a hard-hit ball to their side because they are flatfooted. If the player is flatfooted, she will need more time to get her momentum started forward. Being on the toes and balls of the foot will make the first steps quicker.

2. Preparing Gloves

The glove is the first thing that contacts a batted or thrown ball. Most 8- to 18-years-old players use gloves that are broken in incorrectly or have top strings that are not tight enough to hold the ball in the glove. Many players have broken in the glove so that the pocket is in the webbing of the glove instead of the whole glove being the pocket. Catching the ball anywhere except that one spot is therefore harder. A correctly broken-in glove has the thumb and the little finger slots of the glove lined up from top to bottom when the glove is closed. If they are not, the player is catching with only part of the glove.

Also, if the top of the glove is loose, keeping the ball in the glove when it is caught is harder, especially if the player has to reach or dive for a ball. The looser the glove is, the harder it will be to maintain control and keep it from falling out. Keep the glove strings tight at the top of the glove to prevent this from happening.

There are various ways to break in a glove, but one way is to get it wet (we love rainwater) and place a ball deep in the palm area instead of the webbing. Fold the glove so that the thumb slot and the little finger slot meet from top to bottom. Secure the glove with any type of rope or shoelace and let it dry naturally.

3. Clean Gloves

The glove should be wiped out after every practice or game. It should be kept in a clean glove bag or plastic bag away from dirty shoes and in a clean player's bag. Keep the player's ball bag zipped during games to keep the dirt from the field out of it. Put shoes in a separate place or bag to keep everything clean. Dirt in the bag will transfer to the glove. Keep the player's bag clean. A dirty glove is a slick glove. The ball tends to spin out of dirty gloves. A ball that skids out of the glove is ruled an error, and more games may be lost on errors than are won on hits.

4. Finger Position in the Glove

Most players put one finger in each finger slot. Some leave their index finger out on top of the glove, and that is fine. But consider the size of a female's hand versus the size of a male's hand. Most female's hands are smaller than male's hands. Most males are stronger in the upper body, whereas females have a strong lower body. So a big, loose glove with a spread-out small hand doesn't allow a strong grip on the ball.

A great option is to put the little finger and the ring finger in the last slot together, move the middle finger to the ring finger slot, and move the index finger to the middle finger slot (some like to keep the index finger out of the slot, which is fine).

By moving the fingers down, the glove stays open easier, a better pocket forms, and the thumb slot and little finger slot stay lined up. Keeping the hand out of the glove a little more gives the player a little more range and, most important, the glove will snap shut when the ball goes in, and the ball will stay there. The smaller hand is weaker when spread out to each finger hole and stronger when the fingers are moved down a slot.

At first, the players may say after changing their finger positioning that the two fingers will not fit in the last hole or that it feels weird. But the fingers will fit when that area stretches out a little, and the weird feeling will be forgotten after a short while. So make it mandatory and reassure your players that the new finger positioning will work.

Breaking in the glove correctly and keeping it clean are essential. All the practice in the world won't keep a player from making an error if the glove is poorly broken in or dirty.

5. Preparing Defensively for a Play

The way that players get ready for the next play could be the difference between a hit, an error, or an out. As previously stated, one of the easiest changes players can make is to turn their toes inward rather than outward. In the following sections, keep in mind that the toes are always to be turned inward, putting the players on the balls of their feet.

Good Athletic Position

Players in a good athletic position are on the balls of their feet and have their hands somewhere around the waist and out in front of the body. Players are much quicker to the ball when they use this type of starting position.

Gloves Open Toward the Hitter

Some players have their throwing hand touching or holding on to the glove, which slows their reaction time and makes it hard to react when a ball goes to the side or a hard line drive comes directly to them. Others have the inside of the glove facing themselves or the ground, which doesn't allow enough time to react to a line drive or a ball sharply hit to the side. Have your players hold their hands out toward the hitter with the glove wide open and partially turned to the hitter.

Infield Corners Down With Weight Forward

The infield corners need to be down and ready for a rocket coming their way. These players should be close to the ground with the hands and glove out in front of the body and opened more to the hitter. The player should not have the throwing hand on the glove or have the back of the glove facing the hitter. That positioning will only slow the reaction time to the hot smash. On the pitch, taking a little hop puts the feet in motion and speeds up the player's reaction time. Planting the feet firmly on the ground invites the opposing team to bunt because the player will have a slower reaction time.

Middle Infielders and Outfielders More Upright Than Corner Infielders

Along with having a good athletic starting position, the middle infielders and the outfielders should be standing up slightly rather than crouching so that they can move laterally quicker. They have more ground to cover than the corner infielders do.

When they are crouching and have their gloves near the ground or on their knees, they first have to get up from the crouch before they are able to go for the ball. Standing up more allows them to pivot and go straight to the ball, which could be the difference between a hit and an out.

Also, if they are standing rather than crouching, they can more easily have their feet moving a little versus being planted on the ground. Again, being in motion when the ball is hit makes a lot of difference in the result of the play. The movement can be a small hop on the pitch or just a shift of the feet before the pitch is made. The time wasted getting the body in motion after the ball is hit can be the difference between an out and a hit.

6. Light on the Feet

If you want quicker players, teach them agility. Agility equipment can be purchased or made at home. Teaching the players to be agile and coordinated is well worth the money it takes to purchase the equipment or the time it takes to make it. The players will have better balance, and their center of gravity will feel higher in the body instead of in their feet and legs, which makes them slower. They will learn to move their feet quicker and more efficiently. Players will feel more confident in their playing ability because they will be getting to more balls on defense and will be quicker on the bases on offense.

A great way to start an agility program is to use an agility ladder, cones, jump ropes, and spots and do carioca. Just doing some exercises with agility equipment will help your team with coordination, balance, and quickness.

7. Using Opposition and Follow-Through When Throwing

Many players complain of arm soreness in front of their shoulders when throwing. Players may also have trouble getting the ball to the intended target with much velocity. To learn why, watch three specific areas when your players throw during a warm-up session.

Throwing-Hand Leg on Release of the Ball

Does the player lift the foot of the throwing-hand leg off the ground, or does she maintain contact with the ground and drag the toe. If she drags the toe or leaves that foot in contact with the ground, she will develop arm problems and will not have much zip on the ball. Usually, when the toe doesn't leave the ground, the ball dies before it gets to the target or has a looping trajectory that takes too long to get to the target.

Rotation of Hips

Do the hips rotate from the side of the hip of the catching-hand side pointing to the target to the hip of the throwing-hand side pointing to the target? If the hips do not rotate, the ball will have less zip.

Arms in Opposition

Players should learn opposition. To do this, the player fields the ball and immediately hops so that her glove side is pointing to the target. The glove hand points in the direction of the target, and the hands then switch positions. If the player is right-handed, the left hand points to the target. In the act of throwing, the left hand pulls back and is replaced with the throwing hand. A swimmer does not swim with one arm. A softball player needs to use her arms in opposition, just as a swimmer does.

When the player does all three of these things during the throwing motion, she will not experience soreness in the front of the shoulder because following through takes the stress off that area. The player will also see the velocity on the ball increase and the ball getting to the target much quicker. That is possibly the difference between the runner being out or being safe.

8. Mental Toughness and Relaxation

The mental toughness of players should not be overlooked during the season. An aggressive offense puts pressure on the defense as part of their strategy during the game. The defense has to be mentally prepared to handle that pressure. Practicing against pressure every day is an essential part of a team's fielding practices. The team will follow the coach's lead. If you are positive, determined, organized, and fear no opponent, the players' attitudes will follow that lead.

If you encourage all players during preseason practices and treat all players the same way, the team will act as one unit. Positive reinforcement from the coaching staff results in the players having confidence in their skills. During every drill, you can make or break the mental toughness of the team. You should inspire and support the team by convincing the players that they can play a great defensive game and win the game. Teaching the players the skills and working toward perfecting those skills with positive remarks and actions creates a positive environment. Negative remarks and actions by the coaching staff tear down team unity and mental toughness.

Seek information on activities that the team can use to build mental toughness. Relaxation techniques are useful. Practicing relaxation techniques and using cue words will produce a calming effect on the defense during the stress of a game.

Players can learn mental toughness through their practices and through the type of schedule played during the season. Lazy, easy practices result in stress for players during pressure games. Playing an easy schedule will not prepare players for the more experienced teams. Preparing practices that teach the players something new every day and encourage them to improve will build their confidence and make them stronger mentally. Playing tougher teams during fall practice games and during the early part of the spring season will pay off at the end of the season and during the playoffs. The team will become more experienced and mentally stronger throughout the season.

If a player makes an error and continues to think about it, she will almost certainly make more errors. A simple word or action from you can calm that player and allow her to focus on subsequent plays. By being supportive instead of being harsh, you let her know that errors will happen and that she should blow it off. The player will then stay positive and go on to the next hitter. Major fixes to the defense are done in practices before and after the games. Plays can be discussed if needed, but negative correction should be limited during games. A good action during the game is to look at the player and give her the action of blowing something off your hand. This tells her to blow it off and go on to the next pitch.

After the aforementioned suggestions on the needed fundamentals skills are implemented, practices will run a lot smoother. The players will be getting to more balls, making more plays, and winning more games. The result will be a happy coach and a happy team.

Basic Game Knowledge

Every aspect of the game and any situation that could possibly occur during a game should be discussed and practiced earlier with the players. If you do that, few surprises will happen during the course of a game. Players will automatically recognize what is happening and know how to handle every situation that arises.

The following topics cover situations that the defense may have to handle during a game. These situations need to be incorporated into practices until everyone understands how to handle them.

Preparing for Difficult Field Conditions

In some areas of the country, teams have to play in difficult conditions. Teams need to practice in these conditions and discuss how to play in them to be adequately prepared and mentally acclimated. The attitude of each team member playing in these conditions is a huge factor in being successful.

The playing field may be in subpar condition:

- Not all fields are perfectly maintained in fair territory.
- Not all fields are level.
- Not all fields are free from clumps or rocks.
- Not all fields are maintained properly in foul territory.

Can your team play on fields that have the following conditions?

- Loose or thick dirt
- Hard-packed mud after a rain
- Very hard infields
- Slopes in the field, especially in the outfield
- Holes in the outfield
- Ruts in the outfield or infield
- Obstacles in foul territory such as a tarp or other equipment
- Tall grass or grass clumps in the outfield

Your attitude toward playing under these conditions has to be one of confidence. You need to show this attitude to the players because they will follow your lead. If you complain outwardly about the conditions and act worried or use excuses, the players will notice that and follow your attitude. Of course, you need to make sure that the field is safe to play on, but any negative discussion should be only among coaches.

The players need to survey the field before each game and look for potential problem areas such as holes in the outfield, slopes in the field, grass clumps, and the shape of the infield. The infielders need to check their areas and then smooth and manicure them. Whenever they are playing defense, they should look at their areas for any problem spots like rocks, divots, and uneven areas where the ball could take a bad hop. If players find any problem areas, they need to smooth them out. Preventing problems is easier than reacting to a bad hop.

Whenever possible, have the team practice in substandard conditions. The players need to assess whether the field is sloped, especially whether it slopes downward toward the outfield fence.

For example, the right fielder needs to be able to read the spin of the ball and the slope to be able to cut off the ball. The first baseman needs to learn the best way to play first. Some coaches like the foot on the base early, but some do not.

If a first baseman puts her foot on the base right away before seeing the path of the ball and a late break occurs in the throw, she may be unable to recover and catch the ball or block it from going down the first-base line. Straddling the base in fair territory with the heels about 4 inches (10 cm) from the base and having the body square to the throw is a better way to cover the base, especially with a slope. When the first baseman assesses the path of the ball, she can pop her foot on the base. If the throw goes wild, she can then slide her foot to a different position on the base and prevent the ball from going into the outfield.

Teams must repeatedly practice catching balls in foul territory. You can place an obstacle in their way such as a coach or equipment so that they learn to go around it. Players should practice the technique for approaching a ball close to the fence. They need to find the fence first to avoid running in to it or letting the ball drop because they do not know how far they are from the fence.

You need to realize that hard-packed mud and sliding do not mix well because the runner will stick on that surface. Stealing could be less likely to occur.

Very hard infields will produce high hops on grounders. Have your players practice smacking the ball down to produce a high hop. Most runners will be safe if the ball takes that high bounce.

Playing in Inclement Weather

Different parts of the country have different weather to deal with every year. Can your team play in the following conditions?

- Extreme heat or humidity
- Very bright sunlight
- High skies where lack of clouds can lead to poor depth perception of the ball
- Rain, drizzle, mist
- Wind
- Sleet
- A little snow
- Chilly to very cold conditions
- Playing in layers of clothing, gloves, warm hats, and so on

If possible, take advantage of days when the weather is not ideal and practice in those conditions. If you do not have some of these inclement conditions in your area and will never see them, consider yourself lucky.

If you travel great distances for tournaments, check the weather possible in those areas. For example, if you travel to a tournament and see that the sky is bright blue and cloudless, recognize that the depth perception on a fly ball may be different. Take time before the game to hit the highest fly balls possible to both the outfielders and the infielders. Also, work on the balls that may go between them. Communication is crucial.

Windy days are great for outfield practices. The outfielders have to learn to track the ball that is being carried by the wind or the ball that suddenly dies in the wind. They need to be able to read the flags or know how to throw some grass in the air to check the wind. The outfielders also need to know how to throw a ball with or against the wind.

The same type of practice is also needed in extremely sunny areas. Players need to wear a visor all the time. The sun and the heat can really take a toll over the course of a game. A visor can really help with that. Athletic sunglasses are also needed. Lacking sunglasses, players need to know how to use their hands to block the sun. They need to communicate with their teammates if they lose the ball in the sun, and those players need to be ready to make the play.

Be prepared for extreme heat by having lots of water available as well as wet small towels or bandanas for the players to wear on the field. Sports drinks are recommended only in extreme heat and humidity. On other days, water is fine. Sports drinks are not only costly but also contain a lot of calories that players do not need under normal conditions.

Be prepared for cold weather with windproof, lightweight jackets that can fit under the uniform top, spandex for under the uniform tops and pants, gloves, headbands for the ears, and hand warmers that go in the back pocket or shoes. Players may also need a change of socks in case they get wet.

Being mentally prepared and mentally tough when playing in inclement conditions is imperative. The players have to use mind over matter and focus on the game, not the elements they are playing in.

Thinking Ahead and Reading the Opposition

Before the pitch is even thrown, the players should think about the following:

- They need to judge the speed of the runner, the speed of the ball coming to them, and their own arm strength. Players should then be able to assess whether they can get the lead runner going to the next base. For example, if a fast runner is on first and the ball coming to the fielder is a slow roller, the play is to first. If the runner on first is a medium to slow runner and the ball coming to the fielder is a medium to hard grounder, the fielder who has a good to excellent arm can go for the out at second.

- They can assess the hitter by looking at her stance (open, even, closed), the length and weight of the bat, the hands and knuckle alignment on the bat, the grip on the bat (high, low, wrapped, choked, or long grip), whether the bottom arm is straight or bent, whether the batter is crouched or standing up.

- They should consider the speed of the pitcher and the location of the pitches.

- They should consider the situation—early or late innings, ahead or behind in the game and by how many runs, the number of outs in the inning.

Planning Efficient Practices

Practices need to be efficient so that the players get the maximum number of balls hit or thrown to them in a reasonable amount of time. The coaches need to tell and show the players what to do. Then it is repetition, repetition,

repetition, with the coaches correcting them in a positive manner. Players can lose interest in practices for several reasons.

Unprepared or Unorganized Coaches

Lack of preparation or organization leads to too much lag time between drills and little continuity during the practices. Players will be standing around with no direction from the coaching staff. Mental lapses, lack of trust in the coaches, boredom, and other problems will result. Most players know exactly when a coach is not organized or prepared for the practice.

Coaches should have a plan for the year and a timeline of what they want to accomplish at any given point in the season, especially during the preseason teaching practices.

Writing out the practices on notecards or pages in a clipboard is fine. The players then know that the coach has put some thought into the practices and has a plan in mind. Notecards can fit into a pocket and are easy to refer to.

Standing Around

Incorporating more players into each of the drills keeps the players from losing their focus. Hitting practices, for example, can be extremely boring for the players in the outfield, especially if the pitching is live and the pitcher cannot throw a ball near the strike zone. Have stations where some players can be working on other skills and just a few are shagging the balls.

Not Being Taught Skills and Strategies

Players are hungry to learn how to play softball the correct way instead of just playing and making the same mistakes repeatedly. Players are eager to learn what to do and why it is done that way. Explain why they should perform a skill a certain way. They will then understand and perform the skill better. Also, plan your practices with your timeline in mind.

Negative Coaching

Players react to different types of coaches in various ways, but most players react positively to coaches who

- are organized,
- teach the game and the strategy of the game,
- have disciplined programs,
- are fair with the entire team no matter the skill level,
- explain why they want things done a certain way,
- are willing to admit they may not know an answer but will find out,
- can laugh and cry with the players, and
- are leaders.

Players will not respect coaches who

- are yellers,
- are unorganized and waste time at practices,
- play favorites,
- think they know everything and are not willing to discuss anything,
- are not leaders, and
- embarrass players especially when they have not been taught the skill.

Having the practices planned around a timeline for the season keeps the learning process moving along. The coaching staff then knows whether the learning process is on schedule, ahead of schedule, or behind schedule. Having the practices planned up to the minute keeps the attention of the players throughout those practices and increases learning.

Practices also need to be planned according to the age and skill level of the players. Don't expect a young player to be able to make the plays that an experienced player can make. On the other hand, don't coach an experienced player the way you would coach a younger player. The length and intensity of the practices and the number of balls hit to and thrown by a player all have to be geared to the player's age.

Effective Practice Plans

Teams in most of the country, if they play their games during the spring season, have their preseason practices in a gym. Learning to use every bit of space can be a challenge, as we'll discuss later in the chapter. But many drills can be adapted to various areas if the right equipment is used. Here is a sample preseason practice.

Warm-Ups

On arrival to practice, the players jog around the perimeter of the gym for the number of minutes you desire; less than 15 is recommended. During that time, the players may do the following to practice eye–hand or other coordination skills.

Ball Toss

The leader tosses a ball over her head to the next in line. In turn, she tosses the ball overhead to the next player. When the last person receives the ball, she sprints to the head of the line and tosses the ball over her head to the next player, and the drill continues.

Locomotor Skills

On each side of the gym, players switch to a new locomotor skill that the leader chooses—hop on one foot, do a side slide down one side of the gym

> Tip: A good resource to find locomotor skills is a book about PE in elementary schools. Children should be taught these skills in elementary school, but many are not. Learning these skills is essential in playing any sport at any age.

and switch to the other leg leading down the other side of the gym, high knees, hip kicks, gallops, carioca facing inward and changing to outward, jog backward, and so on.

Reaction and Coordination

- The coach calls out instructions to the players—jog, slide, gallop, and so on to work on their reaction time.
- Have partners do the previous activities tossing a ball or a beanbag underhand to each other. This activity teaches eye–hand coordination and the use of soft hands.

Agility Workouts

Agility workouts are a good way to warm up the players and teach them to be light on their feet and quicker in the movements needed to get to a ball or a base. Many teams use a dynamic warm-up instead of the traditional stretching warm-up in which the team sits in a circle or group.

A typical agility workout consists of the following drills with adjustments made for the age and skill level of the players.

Ladder Drills

Ladder drills will help the player develop quicker feet (be light on the feet), coordination, and balance.

Equipment

Rope ladder

Setup

- One foot in each section
- One foot in and one foot out
- Two feet in each section

Execution

- Jump two feet in and then jump two feet out, alternating for the length of the ladder (figure 8.1a).
- Two feet in going sideways
- Two feet in one at a time and a third step out facing forward (rhythm is in-in-out, in-in-out, and so on) (figure 8.1b)

Coaching Points

- A more advanced version is to use the same rhythm but face sideways, or perpendicular, to the ladder and go to the left for one length and to the right for the second length (figure 8.1*c*).

- When going through a ladder, players often try to look at their feet, which will slow them down and put them off balance. Keep reminding them to stand straight up to keep their balance. The players should work to increase their speed through the ladder. Ladders can be lengthened as the players advance.

- All these drills can be done if time allows during the practice, or a portion of them can be done if time is short. As the team progresses into the more difficult ones, the simple ones can be dropped from the workout.

- Players do all these drills at a speed they can handle at first and build to the quickest speed possible. Lengths of a normal agility ladder can be added if needed.

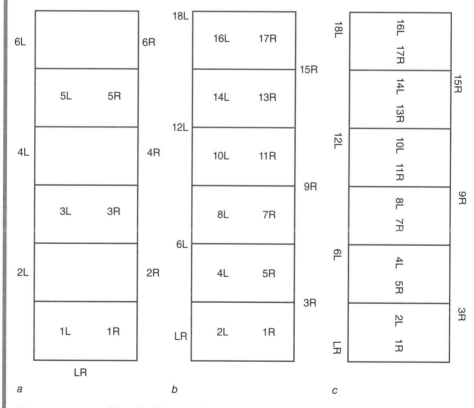

Figure 8.1   Ladder drills: (*a*) alternating in-out; (*b*) in-in-out; (*c*) sideways in-in-out.

Cone Drills, Spot Drills

These drills develop quickness, coordination, and balance.

Equipment

Standard traffic cones of any size and round spots (can be dots or squares) that are flat on the ground.

Execution

- Players use a shuffle step to go through the cones going forward (figure 8.2*a*).
- They use a side shuffle step to go through side first (figure 8.2*b*).
- Facing away from the cones, they go through the cones backward doing a shuffle step (figure 8.2*c*).
- The distance from cone to cone and alignment of the cones can vary for each of the previous drills, or they can be placed in a straight line.
- Stagger the cones so that one is at 5 feet (1.5 m), then 10 feet (3 m), 15 feet (4.5 m), and 20 feet (6 m). Players use any locomotor movement to go to the first cone and back, the second cone and back, and so on. They can use a backpedal to come back to the start line from each length (figure 8.2*d*).

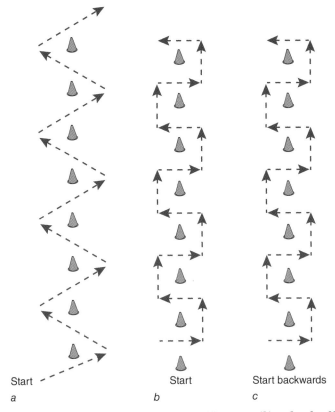

Figure 8.2 Cone drills, spot drills: (*a*) shuffle step; (*b*) side shuffle step; (*c*) backward shuffle step. *(continued)*

- Place the cones in any pattern in a small area. Players again use any locomotor movement to go around each one. They can vary the movements used, or you can call out the movements. Set up two courses and divide players into teams to add a little competition to the workout.

- Space cones about 10 feet (3 m) apart in a straight line. The player faces the first cone, opens her hips and sprints to the second cone, plants and faces the cone, and repeats to the subsequent cones in the same manner. After reaching the last cone, the player pivots and sprints back to the first cone.

- Place numbered cones in a diamond shape. The player starts in the middle of the cones. When you call a number, the player moves to that cone, touches it, and immediately goes back to the center (figure 8.2e). Watch that the player goes directly to the cone without taking extra steps and that the player faces you the entire time.

- For pivot drills, place spots in line A about 3 feet (1 m) apart in a straight line. Place another set of spots in line B about 5 feet (1.5 m) away and place those spots so that they are in line with the halfway mark or one-and-a-half mark of the spots on the other line. The player starts at line A, runs to line B, places the left foot on the spot, pivots, goes to the next spot in line A, places the right foot on the spot, and immediately goes the next spot in line B. The player keeps going to the last spot and uses a blind pivot.

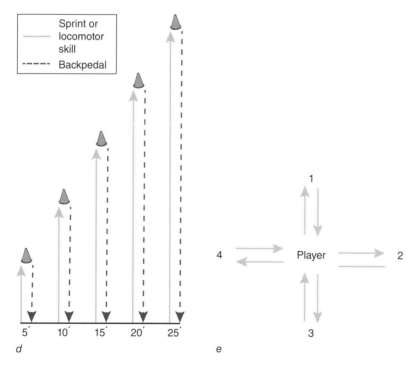

Figure 8.2 *(continued)* Cone drills, spot drills: (*d*) out, backpedal back; (*e*) diamond-shaped drill.

Line Drills

Quick Feet Drills

Equipment

Drills can be done by using any existing line on a gym floor or by using jump ropes placed on the floor.

Setup

Have the players pick any line and stand shoulder-length apart.

Execution

- With their sides to the line, the players hop over the line with one foot as fast as possible, switch to the other foot, and then switch to both feet.
- Facing the line, the players hop over the line as fast as possible.
- Facing the line, the players hop over with one foot followed by the other and then back over with one and then the other, repeating as fast as possible.
- Fast feet—the players run in place as fast as possible. On command, they make quarter turns to 180-degree turns.

Eye–Hand Drills With Conditioning

These drills teach the players to run and catch at the same time. Players develop eye–hand–foot coordination, work on their reaction time to the hit or throw, and improve their acceleration ability when sprinting and getting to the ball.

In and Out Drills

This drill is like suicides, but players catch on the way to the lines and throw the ball back.

Equipment

A glove and ball for each player

Setup

Players are in a line and each has a ball.

Execution

Each player has a ball and gives it to the coach when it's her turn. The coach takes the ball from the player. The player runs to a specific area and receives the ball from the coach. For example, the player runs to a designated spot and breaks left for the throw (figure 8.3*a*). After receiving the ball, the player carries the ball back to the end of the line. Next time up, the player runs and breaks to the right (figure 8.3*b*). Next time up, the player runs straight and receives a throw over her shoulder. Immediately after catching this ball, she throws to the catcher and sprints in to receive a short toss (figure 8.3*c*).

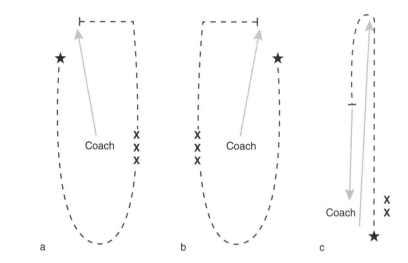

Figure 8.3 In and out drills: (*a*) cut left; (*b*) cut right; (*c*) overhead.

Quick Defense Drills

Setup

Players are in a line with a ball.

Execution

This time the player goes to the designated area, breaks left to receive the ball, and throws it back to the catcher. She then immediately sprints to the right for the catch and returns the ball to the catcher. She then runs straight out for an over-the-shoulder catch and throws the ball to the catcher. Finally, she runs straight in for a short diving catch (figure 8.4).

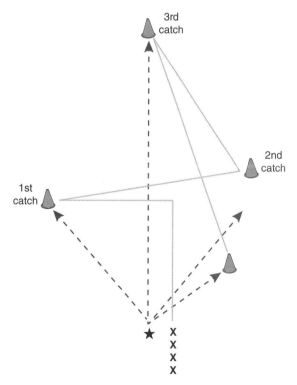

Figure 8.4 Quick defense drills.

Skill Practice

Divide the gym in half and use half for bunting and slapping practice and the other half for fielding practice.

Side A—Outfielders and Pitchers Practice Bunting and Slapping

Drill 1

Four players bunt for a hit off a machine without defense. The rest of the players just shag and return balls to the person at the machine. The players bunting get one pitch for a bunt on the run. The players do this quickly so that they get the idea to be ready to run out of the bunt.

Setup

The person feeding the machine puts a ball in as quickly as possible and continues to feed the machine at a steady pace. Obviously, the feeder has to adapt the speed to the ability of the players who are bunting but will soon come to a good rhythm.

Execution

The first player bunts on the run, runs 5 to 10 steps, and then goes to the end of the line. The second player bunts immediately after the first one and so on.

Coaching Points

- The player should transfer her weight to the front foot when starting her run. The back foot is off the ground on contact.
- The hands on the bat are split so that they are stronger when contacting the ball. The wrist on the bottom hand should be pointed down to make it stronger. The top hand should grip the bat with at least three fingers and the thumb.
- Using fewer fingers makes the hand weaker. When either hand is in a weak position, the player is at higher risk of fouling the ball off against faster pitches.
- The bat should be level and at eye level away from the body.
- The ball is contacted out in front of the body, and the top hand acts as a pivot point. If the player pushes the bottom hand straight out, the ball goes toward first if the batter is right-handed and toward third if the player is left-handed. If the bottom hand is pulled in as far as possible, the ball off a right-handed batter will go toward third and the ball off a lefty will go toward first.
- When a lefty wants to do a drag bunt toward first, it is easier to use just the top hand and take the bottom hand off the bat. The bat in this case needs to be in the high strike area, parallel to the ground. The bottom of the bat and knob should be against the player's forearm for stability.
- After all balls have been used, ideally after at least two buckets of balls, switch to four new players. Each group should practice bunting a couple of times if possible.

Variations

- When all players have bunted numerous times, add a defense. The drill will go slower because the defenders are throwing the ball to first.
- Do the same drill but switch to slapping.
- Do slapping against a defense.

Side B—Infielders and Catchers Do Infield Practice

Drill 1

Setup

Maximize the number of repetitions for each player by alternating hits to third base and shortstop and having the third baseman throw to first and the shortstop throw to second.

Execution

- The players receiving the throws can either put the ball in a bucket or toss to a specific shagger. The hitter put balls in play quickly by hitting to the shortstop as the first fielder is throwing, doing this numerous times (figure 8.5a).
- The hitter switches to hitting to the second baseman who throws to third and to the first baseman who throws to the shortstop covering second. The hitter needs to pay attention to where the players are so that no one is in a throwing lane. Repeat until all players have had their workouts (figure 8.5b).

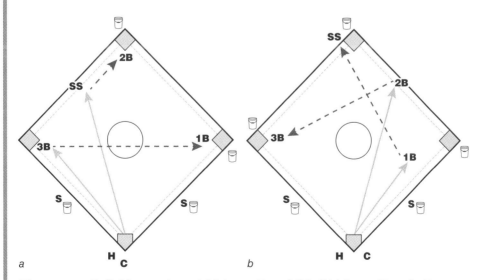

Figure 8.5   Infield practices: (*a*) hit to 3B and SS; (*b*) hit to 2B and 1B. *(continued)*

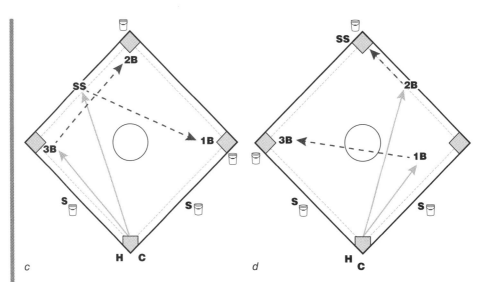

Figure 8.5 *(continued)* Infield practices: (*c*) hit to 3B and SS; (*d*) hit to 2B and 1B.

- The hitter switches to hitting to the third baseman who now throws to second and to the shortstop who now throws to first (figure 8.5*c*).
- The hitter switches to hitting to the second baseman who now throws to the shortstop covering second and to the first baseman who throws to third (figure 8.5*d*).

Drill 2

Players field various types of hits.

Execution

The coach hits to the infielders by hitting hard grounders, soft grounders, line drives, balls over the head, bunts, short hops, backhand shots, hits up the middle, hits in the gaps, hits down the lines, foul-ball pop-ups, foul-ball line drives, and balls that require players to throw on the run.

Coaching Point

For a couple of these kinds of balls, throwing the ball to the desired area is easier than hitting the ball with a bat. Too much time is wasted trying to hit the ball in shallow areas like just over first or third, so you can just throw it there for better accuracy. Keeping the practice moving is extremely important in keeping the players involved mentally.

Players switch to the other side of the gym. For side 2A, infielders and catchers do the slap and bunt drills described earlier. For side 2B, outfielders practice fielding (because the gym probably has a low ceiling, the high fly ball drills have to be outside).

Drill 1

Outfielders and pitchers work on line drives, bloops, two-person tweeners, foul balls, grounders, and throwing to the various bases. Emphasis should be on getting the ball in to the infielders quickly and accurately.

Situational Practice

Open the curtain that divides the room and bring the team back together for a situational practice. While working on situational plays, practicing with pressure is extremely important to simulate game situations.

Drill 1

The infielders work on grounders and situations. The outfielders, extra pitchers, and catchers are runners. Tell the runners to be aggressive but smart. This drill puts pressure on the fielders and gives them a better idea of how quick they need to be to get the out. They also need to think ahead and be ready for the second and third plays. You can hit the ball anywhere at any time to cover all situations. You can hit singles, doubles, and balls that ricochet off the walls. Runners should purposely get into rundown when you call it. You can put runners on bases to work on various situations.

   This drill is also helpful for the runners. By trying to push the infielders, they learn when to stay, when to go, when to take an extra base, and how to be aggressive.

Drill 2

The outfielders work on line drives, bloops, balls down the line, balls off the fence (wall), tweeners, and so on. Infielders, extra catchers, and pitchers run the bases. Extra outfielders take their throws at the bases and home. The runners work on being aggressive, breaking off the bases to draw throws, and tagging up and advancing to the next base. You can put runners on base to work on situations. To take it a step further, when the ball is thrown to the catcher to get a runner, she can then throw the ball to another base, simulating the batter or baserunner taking an extra base. From there, the ball can be thrown to other bases as well. For example, the ball goes to the catcher, she make a tag and throws to second, the player there makes a tag and throws to third, and the third baseman makes a tag and throws home. After the initial throw to the catcher, the runners are imaginary, but the fielders get to practice thinking ahead, making a tag, pivoting, and going quickly to the next play.

   Having players practice numerous skills in the same drill is beneficial. More players are involved, and the players have to go on to the next play, work on a tag play, and quickly go on to the next play. You can call out the base to go to next, and the players have to react.

   Finish the practice with a short game with a pitcher. Put runners on bases for situations. Work on steals, delay steals, squeezes, and breaking off bases to put pressure on the defense, including the pitcher and catcher.

All players need encouragement and positive feedback, but they also need direction and discipline. The best way to have effective learning at practices is to be organized, positive, and definite in the way you give directions. Self-assured, confident instruction lets the players know that the coaching is strong. They will follow.

Chapter 9

Developing the Pitcher and Catcher

Connie Clark

Many coaches believe that the game of fastpitch softball revolves around dominance in the pitching circle. I agree with this thought to a certain extent, but it really comes down to the battery mates, their connection, and their execution of the game within the game. The relationship between the pitcher and catcher is unique. Although the duo is part of a team, each game, each inning, and each pitch begin with them.

Three areas are important to zero in on when developing the pitcher and catcher: attacking the physical demands, developing a mentality for success, and mastering the art of deception. The three areas can be broken down so that the battery mates can learn the importance of each piece as it relates to their own personalities and strengths.

I would be remiss by jumping right into our specific subject without sharing something that is critical to a team's development and ultimately the success of the battery. When first starting the program at the University of Texas, specific words came up repeatedly, whether we were teaching a skill at practice, setting academic goals, creating our culture, or developing life skills. Words such as trust, teamwork, integrity, persistence, belief, respect, and discipline were often echoed in pregame speeches, in huddles, and in the locker room by both athletes and coaches. As we worked through the first two years (a club year and varsity status in year 2), it became evident that our foundation and culture were being formed.

Our foundation became DIRT, which stands for discipline, integrity, respect, and teamwork. This acronym became what we stood for. One of the greatest joys of being a coach is identifying the personality and strength of a team each year. Although we may have to motivate each group a little differently and each group will designate their specific standards for DIRT, our foundation is what we live by every day and every year.

DIRT allows our staff and team to attach expectations to what we want to happen on and off the field, as well as in the classroom. Having a solid foundation is a must for any program or business. Developing your overall team or organization according to your foundation will run a parallel course to preparing your pitchers and catchers physically, mentally, and in the art of deception.

Physical Demands

Today we live in a specialty world. Athletes can pay an instructor to teach them anything and everything related to the game: pitching, hitting, fielding, strength, speed, agility, sport psychology, and so on. Our equipment is specialized to perform at the highest level possible. We use high-tech video to compare, emulate, and fix physical mechanics. Technology and specialization is incredible, but athletes as well as coaches can become consumed with the pursuit of perfection. Perfect mechanics don't constitute desired results. The game of softball is not about being perfect; it's about adjusting and compensating. It's about focusing on what we can control and staying true to the development of individual strengths as opposed to consuming ourselves with our weakness.

Verbiage and the Why Factor

Week 1 in the bullpen consists of understanding verbiage that pitchers and catchers have been taught by previous coaches. Your verbal cues may have meanings that differ from those of another coach, so you need to establish clear communication right away. You should also talk through the why factor by asking questions and listening intently to the answers of your athletes. Some athletes can tell you why they do a particular move or skill, but others may not. Our athletes need to know why they do something a certain way; they should be able to connect the dots. This understanding will increase their overall skill set and accelerate the learning process.

These early bullpen meetings should be active learning sessions, not just conversations. As specific verbiage regarding physical mechanics is being established, athletes should have a ball or gear in hand so that they can show you the skill as well as articulate it. This approach puts them in a confident and open-minded position, and you and the athletes can quickly get on the same page. The session can also address two other key pieces: understanding what type of learners the athletes might be (feel, visual, audio) and establishing rapport between you and the athletes.

Expectations

During the initial week with your pitchers and catchers, you should clearly outline expectations regarding the battery. They should know that there will be a commitment to develop them physically, mentally, and in the art of deception. And those aspects should be attacked in that order. Sure, some of the mentality and deceptive pieces will surface as you develop them physically, but the puzzle should be put together gradually.

Key Physical Components

The physical pieces can be overwhelming to the athletes if you try to establish too many things at one time. Keep it simple and follow a teaching sequence so that the pitcher and catcher can master the critically important base components. The following list will help you set up a sequence.

Pitcher

- Practice routine—warm-up, focus catch, and dailies
- Grip selection and finger pressure
- Power line, body position, arm slot and spacing, arm whip and sequencing
- Presentation, load, and explode
- Deep breath
- Body language

Catcher

- Practice routine—warm-up, focus catch, and dailies
- Stance
- Footwork, arm action, and transition
- Receiving from the pitcher, framing
- Blocking
- Receiving from fielders, tag and force
- Body language (demanding a pitch location and projecting leadership)

The aforementioned bullet points can be plugged into a teaching sequence over the span of three weeks (figure 9.1). This preseason phase can serve as a framework to build on. Verbiage, practice routines, and basic physical mechanics can be established.

Figure 9.1   Three-Week Training Sessions

Week 1: Three 40-Minute Sessions

	Activity	Length (minutes)
	Day 1	
P & C	Establish warm-up and focus catch	20
P	Compare verbiage while doing spin work; focus on four keys	20
C	Stance and framing discussion and tennis ball drill	20
	Day 2	
P & C	Warm-up, focus catch, and introduce dailies	25
P	Spin work, verbiage, and whys; focus on four keys	15
C	Tennis ball drill and introduce blocking	15
	Day 3	
P & C	Warm-up, focus catch, dailies	22
P	Full-motion mechanics (present, load, and explode)	10
C	Tennis ball and blocking drills	10
P & C	Catcher receives from pitcher; each has respective focus	8

Week 2: Three 40-Minute Sessions

	Activity	Length (minutes)
	Day 1	
P & C	Warm-up, focus catch, dailies, and introduce long toss	25
P	Grip and finger pressure discussion, spin work, and full motion into net	15
C	Footwork, arm action, transition introduction and drills	15
	Day 2	
P & C	Warm-up, focus catch	15
P & C	Breathing and body language expectations	10
P & C	Catcher receives for pitcher; videotape the session	15
	Day 3	
P & C	Watch video from day 2; analyze breathing and body language	10
P & C	Warm-up, focus catch, and dailies	20
P & C	Pair up and spin work only with respective focus	10

Week 3: Three 40-Minute Sessions

	Activity	Length (minutes)
	Day 1	
P & C	Warm-up, focus catch, dailies	20
P	Spin and warm up half of pitches with a manager or coach	12
P	Location workout: the clock	8
C	Receiving from fielder discussion, tag and force	8
C	Drills: catcher makes throws to all bases; return throws mix tag and force plays	12
	Day 2	
P & C	Warm-up, focus catch	15
P & C	Pair up, spin, and warm up all pitches	25
	Day 3	
P & C	Warm-up, focus catch, dailies	20
P & C	Pair up, spin, and warm up half of pitches (opposite of day 1) and location workout	20

P = pitcher; C = catcher.

Establishing Practice Routines

Getting the body and the mind ready for practice or game day is a controllable act that can set the tone for the rest of the day. One of my favorite books, *The Slight Edge* by Jeff Olsen (2005), talks about turning simple disciplines into success. A well-designed warm-up and practice routine is indeed a simple discipline. A quotation from the book states, "Position your daily actions so time is working for instead of against you. Because time will either promote you or expose you." This idea relates directly to a productive warm-up routine. We want it ingrained into the athlete so that she does not have to think, although warming up should be a mindful act. When done with a high level of focus over a long period, warming up will pay dividends.

First, we warm up the body by going through a series of dynamic stretches, sprints, and arm exercises with bands. We then move into overhand throwing, gradually lengthening it out. After the athlete's arms are loose, they do a round of focus catch. This activity entails partnering up and doing 20 throws (10 each) with complete focus. The goal is to be as quick as possible by using efficient footwork, throwing to the chest of the receiver, and having full concentration.

The final piece of our warm-up routine is called dailies, a series of foundational skills that allow quick and efficient repetitions. Because the players do these each day, the number of opportunities over a season is significant. Pitchers, catchers, and the other positional players have their own set of skills. Typically, athletes have four skills, and they do five repetitions of each before moving on to the next one. For example, a catcher's skills might be blocking, framing, footwork for pick plays, and tag plays. Five to eight minutes may be needed to execute the entire set.

Basic Mechanics

The physical components of the three-week plan include the mechanics that are vital to building a solid foundation. The nine opportunities outlined in figure 9.1 do this. Mechanics also touch on mentality, which presents itself through body language and opens the subject about deception.

Demanding Physicality

How does your catcher demand a pitch when she is receiving? She should use assertive body language, maybe with glove movement or a nod of the head. The gesture maybe subtle, but it can make all the difference in the world for a pitcher's confidence and the connection between the two. Additionally, conversations regarding the art of deception will come into play. For example, presentation and grip selection for the pitchers can be problematic areas that can tip opposing teams or coaches. For catchers, throwing transitions on pick plays should be decoyed as well as possible. We cover mentality and deceptive topics in depth later in the chapter.

Breathing

The final and possibly the most critical physical skill taught during the initial phase is the effect of proper breathing. Athletes often don't understand the physiological benefits of taking a deep cleansing breath in the midst of a stressful situation. This mechanism should also be part of their prepitch routine. Deep breathing releases tension and keeps the pace and rhythm of the pitcher's mechanics in check. Breathing is a skill that needs to be addressed and practiced in the bullpen. It is so important that it warrants being plugged into the core physical mechanics within the initial teaching phase.

Individual Strengths

As the athletes work through their respective physical pieces during this short period, individual strengths will become evident. The goal becomes to develop strengths to become stronger and attack weaknesses to become better. Cat Osterman, who pitched and rewrote the record book at Texas, is a two-time Olympian, currently competes in the National Professional Fastpitch league, and has the best dropball in the world. Her physical makeup, or DNA as we like to say, indicates that she is more natural coming over the top of the ball versus coming under it. Sure, she should develop cutting under the riseball enough to change the eyes of a hitter, but we didn't force her to become something she is not.

I am often asked which pitch to teach first and in what order to proceed. The saying goes, "A hitter's job is to be on time, and the pitcher's job is to disrupt that timing." Therefore, our next priority is to identify an off-speed pitch. For Osterman, our first choice was to tweak hand positions and grips that feel natural coming over the top, like the off-speed drop and a flip change.

As you move past the initial three weeks and progress into the next phase of development, take what the athlete gives you and focus three-quarters of your time on her strengths.

Mentality for Success

Sports performance specialist Dr. Ken Ravizza, one of my mentors, has a saying: "Ain't no use worrying if it's in your control, and if it isn't in your control, then ain't no use worrying."

Getting your pitcher and catcher to hone in on controllable items within the game is the first step in developing the right mind-set. Our game has many uncontrollable pieces, such as weather, umpire decisions, defensive blunders, and offensive miracles. I call them miracles because crazy results can occur when a hitter contacts the ball. A pitcher may execute her intent, but a check swing can wreak havoc. The teaching point is to celebrate the process and the execution of the pitch. The other point is to respect the game, because results and miracles are out of our control. The mental game separates good athletes from great ones.

Routines and Strategies

I was fortunate to have access to Dr. Ravizza while I attended Cal State Fullerton and pitched for Hall of Fame coach Judi Garman. At Fullerton, Ken, a professor on campus, worked with our team as well as with Augie Garrido's baseball squad. He has worked with a number of MLB teams as well as Olympic athletes in several sports. Ravizza is an expert in his field. His book *Heads Up Baseball* lays out the process for playing the game one pitch at a time. He helps us understand that mental routines must be developed just as physical ones are. He uses a simple cycle to help athletes move through their mental routine:

Self-control—plan—trust

A pitcher needs to be in control of herself before she can attempt to control her performance. At times, moving through the cycle is easy because things are going smoothly. When challenging situations occur during a game, the same process may become a little more intensive. A prepitch mental checklist would look like this:

Self-Control: Take a deep breath.

Plan: Get the signal from the catcher and develop a quick reactionary thought about the desired location and result.

Trust: Turn the brain off and deliver the pitch.

During stressful situations, when athletes may struggle to gain self-control quickly, mental strategies can serve as an important addition to the recommended cycle. Even if a miracle happens, strategies can prevent a big inning from occurring because a pitcher can regroup quickly and keep momentum on her side. The following strategies are useful in keeping players calm and focused.

Deep Breathing and Physical Release

We talked earlier about the importance of breathing. A pitcher who cannot control her breathing will never be able to control anything else. At times of high duress, the use of a physical release may be important as well. This action can be as simple as grabbing a fistful of dirt and tossing it. The act symbolizes letting go of the previous pitch or situation and moving the focus to the next pitch.

Focal Points

A focal point takes the athlete to an external focus as opposed to being stuck internally. When things get crazy in the middle of an inning, a focal point becomes something to rely on. A letter on the scoreboard, the flag, or a quotation or image written on the player's glove can all serve to get the pitcher or catcher out of her own head. The player recognizes that things are speeding up, but she has the ability to slow it back down by taking a little extra time to use her focal point.

Positive Self-Talk

Positive self-talk such as "We've got this" or "She's mine" will keep the pitcher in an attack mentality, which is what we want. Using a cue word for each pitch is another piece that Dr. Ravizza passed along to me. At times, a pitcher overthinks her mechanics and becomes overwhelmed by having too many teaching cues in her head. Have the pitcher come up with one word for each pitch. This simple plan can help her mechanically. My trigger word on the curve was "compact." It is crazy I remember that 30 years later, but the word reminded me to do the physical things within my control to make the best attempt at my desired result. The coach and catchers should know these words and use them when needed.

Strategies need not be used after every pitch and may not be needed in a given inning. The mental and physical pieces work simultaneously to keep the battery rolling along, but under duress the athlete may need to rely on something more than her routine.

Attacking the Hitter

Although attacking a hitter sounds purely physical, I placed it in the mental section because throwing your best stuff on any given day starts between the ears. Young pitchers typically expect their bodies to feel 100 percent every day and to have full velocity as well as great movement. Unfortunately, for a number of reasons they will not be at their best every day, so teaching them to embrace this reality is important. The pregame warm-up should include a discussion regarding strengths for the day. The pitcher needs to recognize what she has to work with on a given day versus stuff that doesn't feel great.

After the game is underway, the focus for our battery is to get ahead in the first three pitches. We absolutely want to be at a one-ball, two-strike count at this point. Hitting statistics jump significantly with a two-ball, one-strike situation. Many coaches want to get ahead on the first pitch, but I think that the first pitch can serve as a way to gather information. Was the batter overaggressive? If she took the pitch, how did she track the ball? What was her body position like? This information can set the tone as to how we set up the hitter the rest of the way. The pitcher's strengths, a hitter's susceptibilities, and the game scenario are all part of the process as well.

The Art of Deception

Deception is a component of pitching that is sometimes left to chance. What I mean by that is that pitchers have different levels of deceptive DNA that coaches cannot teach. The idea can be tough to explain, but when you see it, you know exactly what it is. For instance, when you line up two pitchers side by side, one may hide the ball in her backswing, causing it to disappear from the hitter's eyes for a longer time than it does for the other pitcher. This ability is based on flexibility and the physical makeup of the pitcher. You wouldn't necessarily attempt to teach this to a pitcher, but you sure like to see it on the recruiting trail.

Using the Clock

Pitchers and catchers can be taught to disguise physical elements in several other areas. Earlier in the chapter, two problematic areas for pitchers were mentioned: grip selection and initial movement and presentation. Pitchers often think they need to use a different grip for each pitch they throw, which can make them susceptible to base coaches who can read finger or hand positions. The grip is the vehicle to impart the best spin, but pitchers may want to play around with several options to see whether they can settle on using the same one for a number of their pitches. The location workout listed as the clock in figure 9.1 (week 3, day 1) is a good way to introduce using the same grip to produce different breaks just by loading the finger pressure slightly different. Picture a clock (old school with the numbers on its face) and visualize a right-handed pitcher throwing a curveball that breaks left and hits the nine o'clock spot. For the next two pitches she has to get a slightly different finger pressure load to hit the eight o'clock location and then the seven o'clock location. The same grip is used for all three pitches, but with a different load we get to cross multiple planes fairly easily. Yes, hand positions will be different coming into the prerelease zone, but at that point it will be very late for a coach to pick it up.

Deceiving With Presentation

Opposing teams can often pick apart a pitcher on the initial movement or as she begins her presentation. This problem is usually caused by tempo or body position issues. Pitchers need to make every pitch look the same. Doing this takes practice, of course, but a good tool is video analysis. Athletes often cannot feel what they are doing wrong, but seeing it pulls everything together.

Catchers need to work on hiding signals as they pass them along to the pitcher, and they must be aware of their setup in regard to location. The one area that separates outstanding catchers at the higher level is the ability to decoy on a pick play. The catcher must be quick, but she can also disguise her intent by what she does physically. She can do a quick snap throw from her knees to pick at first or third base, as well as keep the same tempo on her throw back to the pitcher yet slip it past and connect with the second baseman at second.

Game-Day Preparation

Now that we have attacked the physical demands, touched on mentality expectations, and discussed the importance of deception, we are ready to plan for game day. Because we used a systematic approach and laid the foundation for our battery, game-day preparation and game day itself become like an exam, albeit a fun one.

To make sure we are as prepared as possible leading into game day, we use a checklist to assist in planning bullpen and practice sessions. Here is a list with a short explanation for each.

Build Pitch Counts

Working backward from game day, establish a gradual buildup on the number of pitches placed into workouts. During the initial three-week program we discussed earlier, pitch counts would never get over 25.

Following that initial window, our goal is to do two light workouts with a pitch count of 25 to 30 and two heavy workouts of 60 pitches each in a given week. Three of the four workouts would have a live hitter in the box to build confidence leading into game day. One of the heavy days can include getting the pitcher fatigued by doing work on a stationary bike between sets (six sets of 10 pitches). This plan simulates an actual game of 80 to 120 pitches without doing that many arm rotations.

System for Signals

I am asked often whether the catcher should call the game or the coach should call signals in from the dugout. My response is always the same: It depends on personnel. If we have the right mix, such as a veteran catcher and an experienced pitcher, I like the battery to use a scouting report and do the pitch calling themselves. If we need to call pitches from the dugout because of a personnel piece, we are always grooming the catcher for this job. Catchers should think, not just relay a signal. This idea applies to pitch calling as well as pick plays and defensive shifts, which should be covered as well. Figure this out early and apply your system in practice and scrimmages leading into game day so that communication and tempo are clear.

Time-Outs

Using time-outs may seem trivial, and you may not think about adding the process to a game-day practice checklist. But time-outs can be game-changing moments, so practicing them is important. Do you want the entire defense to come together, or just the battery? If the time-out is for the battery only, what does the rest of the defense do? Do you want to walk with your catcher out to your pitcher to get a brief thought from her before the meeting? How do you use a time-out to make a pitching change? Do you point to the bullpen and have the current pitcher wait to give the ball directly to her replacement? Last and most important, what message are you or the catcher conveying by calling the time-out?

Simulate Pressure

Simulating pressure will be the most important thing on your checklist. You should create bullpen sessions and live scenarios that challenge your battery physically, mentally, and on their deceptive pieces. Here are some ways to create pressure:

- Scrimmage and place runners so that the battery has to pitch accordingly for the desired result (ground ball to the left side because a runner is at third with less than two outs).
- Scrimmage with the bases loaded and a full count on the hitter. Use a point system (minus for walks and plus for strikeouts and groundouts).
- Hire an umpire and ask her or him to make random bad calls on purpose to improve your players' focus on mentality.
- During live scenarios, have a station of athletes behind home plate or in the coaches' box area trying to pick pitches. Video this drill so that pitchers can view it later.

Charts

Although we live in a digital world, electronic devices are not allowed in the dugout on game day. Therefore, we use a simple one-page chart (figure 9.2) that includes called pitch, location, actual location, and result for each at-bat.

Some coaches like to gather more information, but I like to chart only what we will use directly with the battery on game day or in practice. The chart is a quick reference for them to look over while our team is on offense. We typically use the chart when reviewing video following a game as well.

Strength and Conditioning

Using specific strength programs for pitchers and catchers is a hot topic. Our strength coach Lance Sewell works with our team as well as with University of Texas baseball. He is one of the best in the business. His philosophy about training is "We want to enhance the ability to play the game by improving general fitness and athletic ability as well as reduce risk of injury." He and I talk about the importance of having a framework and incorporating a mentality for success whether we are on the field or in the weight room.

The following training principles are the core of what our pitchers' and catchers' workouts are built on.

- **Conditioning the entire body**. The pitcher's throwing mechanism starts within the legs and trunk. Forces are initiated in the legs, transferred to the upper body through the trunk, and finally applied to the ball by the hands and fingers.
- **Training of movements, not training of muscles**. Movements are sequential, and movements are explosive. A high level of force, applied quickly, is required.
- **Training for muscle balance**. Strength training is not about bulking up, but balancing both sides of the body.
- **Training for performance, not capacity**. Emphasize quality of effort rather than quantity.
- **Resting and recovering**. Gains are achieved during periods of recovery. Often ignored, rest is the most important piece.

Figure 9.3 shows a specific training regimen put together by Sewell that incorporates the listed training principles. The order of exercises significantly influences the effectiveness of the training session. Large, multijoint power exercises are placed early in the training session because these exercises are crucial for development and the athlete has a minimal amount of fatigue. The general flow of exercises then alternates between upper-body and lower-body exercises or push and pull exercises.

Route for Success

Most athletes, including pitchers and catchers, often try to define success through results. Although results serve a purpose in teaching and can create motivation, athletes need a well-planned route for success. Defining

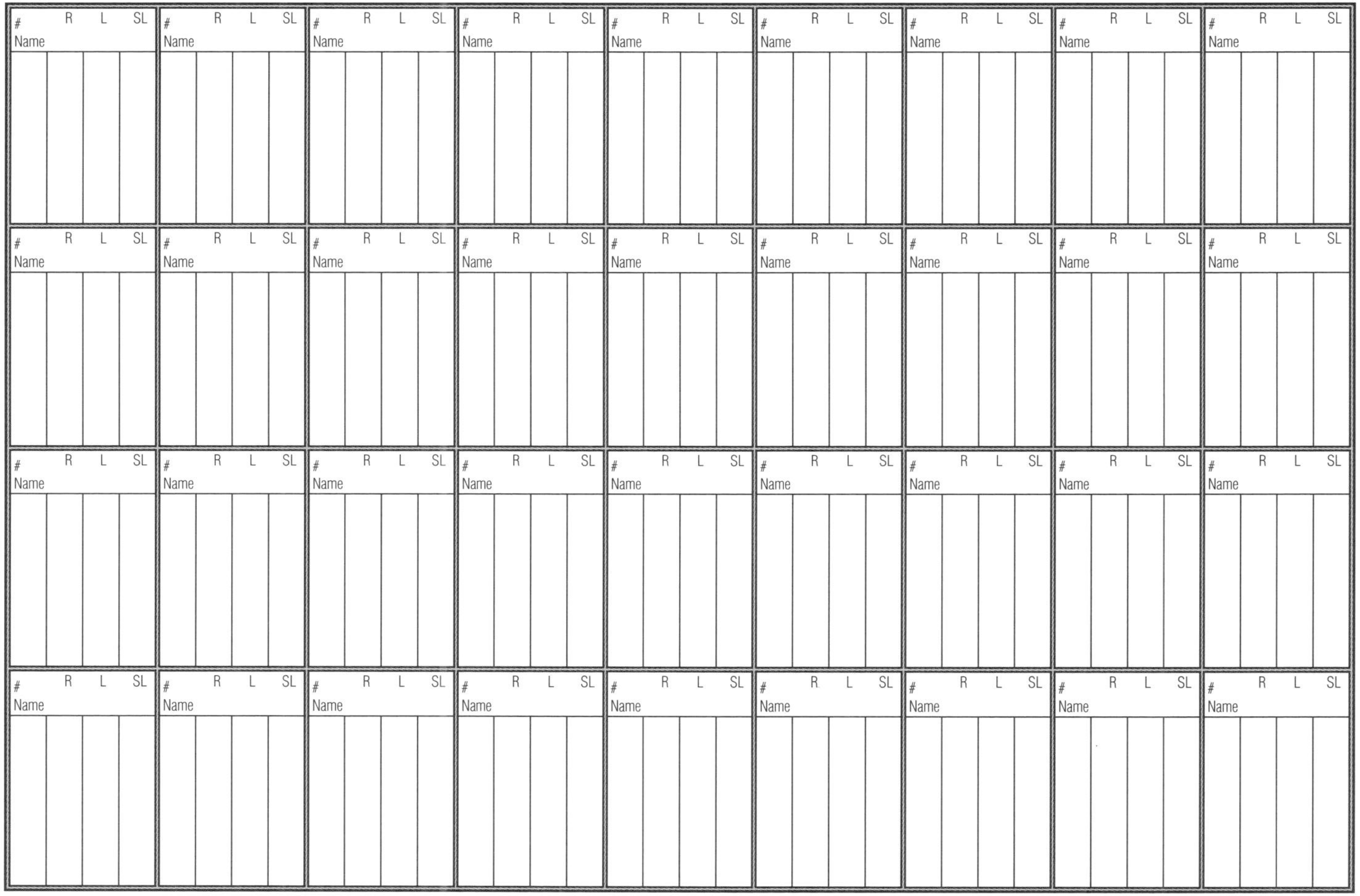

Figure 9.2 Sample pitching chart.

Day 1

Phase / Block:	Foundation			
Emphasis	Base			
	#N/A			Maxes
	#N/A			
	#N/A			

Core	Sets	Reps	Load	Weight
Mini band - lower	1	12	blue	
Mini band - upper	1	10	green	
Med ball rotation and twist	1	10	6	

	Exercise – Day 1	%	Reps	Load	Weight
1 Olympic lift	Hang clean (use 15 kg bar)	50%	5		38.5
		55%	5		42.35
		60%	5		46.2
		65%	5		50.05
2 Olympic lift	Clean pull	70%	5		53.9
		70%	5		53.9
		75%	5		57.75
		75%	5		57.75
3 Vertical pull	Chin up (based on absolute strength)		6		
			6		
			6		
4 Horizontal push	Push up (based on absolute strength)		6		
			6		
			6		
5 Uni-leg	Step up (based on absolute strength)		6		
			6		
			6		
6 Post-chain	Barbell RDL	60%	6		46.2
		65%	6		50.05
		70%	6		53.9

Day 2

Back squat (lbs)	275	
Front squat (lbs)	192.5	#N/A
1 leg squat (lbs)	151.25	#N/A
Power clean (kg)	77	#N/A
Bench press (lbs)	135	

Core	Sets	Reps	Load	Reps	Weight
Mini band - lower	1	12	blue	5	
Mini band - upper	1	10	green	5	
Med ball rotation and twist	1	10	6	5	

	Exercise – Day 2	%	Reps	Load	Weight
1 Squat	Back squat	50%	5		
		60%	5		
		65%	5		
		70%	5		
		75%	5		
		75%	5		
2 Horizontal push	Bench press	50%	6		
		55%	6		
		60%	6		
		65%	6		
		65%	6		
3 Horizontal pull	1 Arm dumbbell row (based on absolute strength)		6		
			6		
			6		
4 Uni-leg	Lateral lunge (based on absolute strength)		6		
			6		
			6		
5 Post-chain	Rhomboid (based on absolute strength)		8		
			8		
			8		
6 Post-chain	Glute hamstring raises		6		BW
			6		BW
			6		BW

Day 3

Core	Sets	Reps	Load	Weight
Mini band - lower	1	12	blue	
Mini band - upper	1	10	green	
Med ball rotation and twist	1	10	6	

	Exercise – Day 3	%	Reps	Load	Weight
1 Olympic lift	Hang clean (use 15 kg bar)	50%	5		38.5
		55%	5		42.35
		60%	5		46.2
		65%	5		50.05
2 Olympic lift	Snatch pull	70%	5		53.9
		70%	5		53.9
		75%	5		57.75
		75%	5		57.75
3 Vertical pull	Pull up (based on absolute strength)		6		
			6		
			6		
4 Horizontal push	Push up (based on absolute strength)		6		
			6		
			6		
5 Uni-leg	3 Position lunge (based on absolute strength)		9		
			9		
			9		
6 Post-chain	Single leg RDL (based on absolute strength)		6		
			6		
			6		

Figure 9.3 Sample of week 1 for a fall semester training plan.

a foundation, developing standards, being challenged to develop physical skills, and acquiring a competitive mentality are all part of the journey. Certainly, these factors aid in the development of pitchers and catchers, but those who absorb the lessons along the way and consistently cycle through the self-control–plan–trust model will end up using it in all facets of their lives. This process is significant and can be the difference in mastering life in general.

During the time a coach has to develop the battery, many trials and tribulations will arise. Patience will be tested, and confidence will wane. By staying true to the standards, coming back to work with creative ideas, having an open mind, and being understanding, a coach can lead, serve, and prepare young athletes for life after the game. The joy is that we get to teach these life skills through an amazing game.

Chapter 10

Perfecting Position Play

Bill Gray and Melissa Chmielewski

Pitching and hitting may get the big headlines, but defense is where the excitement happens on the softball field. Teams can gain momentum on a great diving play by an outfielder, a 6-4-3 double play, a ball speared out of the air by a diving third baseman that doubles off a runner, or a ball thrown from the outfield by a relay that guns down a runner at the plate. I get goose bumps just thinking about it.

Getting those goose bumps takes endless hours of repetition on the basic skills of our game—throwing and catching. Throwing and catching in all phases of infield and outfield play, along with proper alignment during relays, rotations during bunt coverages, and backup responsibilities of all types make the defensive side of the game exciting. Proper throwing mechanics is a critical part in every play made in softball, and it must be worked on at practice every day.

Basic throwing mechanics include

- opening the front hips and shoulder (opening the door) (figure 10.1*a*)
- proper height of front and back elbow (figure 10.1*b*)
- hand position of the throwing arm being palm away from the target (figure 10.1*c*)
- extension and pull of the front arm, and
- release point, wrist snap, and follow-through with the body (closing the door, figure 10.1*d*).

Figure 10.1 *(a)* Opening the door, *(b)* proper height of front and back elbow, *(c)* hand position of the throwing arm, *(d)* closing the door.

Photos courtesy of Jennifer Gray.

Throwing should be more important to your program than playing catch or warming up. Your throwing program should be a planned portion of every practice—knee drills with emphasis on wrist snap and follow-through, four-count throwing in a slow, meticulous manner, individual position throws, simulated game movements, and throwing to targets. The following six skills are essential to any throwing program:

1. Position throws
2. Team throwing

3. Daily dozens
4. Knee throws and wrist snaps
5. Four-count throwing
6. Long toss (everyone, emphasizing leg drive)

Position Throws

Every position has specific throws. Find the throws that are important for each position and have players do repetitions of each of those throws after they loosen up their arms.

Middle Infielders

- Forehand flips—make sure that the body moves toward the target and the follow-through does not get above the waist.
- Backhand flips—watch the follow-through and make sure that it remains parallel with the ground; the throw will follow the angle of the arm.

Corners

- Bunts to the plate—make sure that the body moves toward the target and that the follow-through does not get above the waist.
- Bunts with throws to first base, second base, and third base—field the ball with the body open to the target.

Catchers

- Pickoff throws to bases—point shoulder to the target and follow through.

Outfielders

- Crow hops—watch where they are fielding the ball (near front foot) and look for weight transfer.
- Long hops to the bases—ball should hop 15 to 20 feet (4.5 to 6 m) in front of the catcher so that she has a play.

Team Throwing

The only person in our game who throws to a stationary target is the pitcher. Even then, the catcher moves after making a signal, so athletes need to be used to throwing to a moving target or one that has moved. These drills should include movement of the target and possibly the thrower. Four-corner or star drills, rundown throws, and drills that include an agility ladder are a few of our favorites.

Four Corners

Equipment

- Four bases
- One to four softballs

Setup

Split up players evenly at each base. Start with one ball at home plate. Dictate which way the ball is thrown and whether the thrower follows the ball (runs to the next line or stays at the base).

Execution

The receiver at the first target calls for the ball. The thrower throws to the target and runs to the end of the next line. The receiver catches and makes a tag (if appropriate, with footwork), moves the ball on to the next base, and follows her throw to the next base (figure 10.2). Continue as long as you like, changing direction as necessary. To increase difficulty and improve communication, add a second ball at second base (athletes should stay at the base where they start).

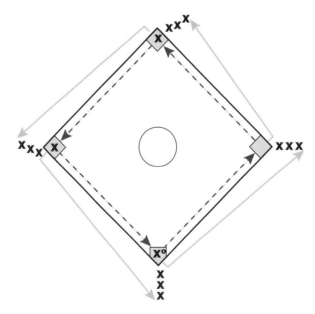

Figure 10.2   Four corners.

Star Drill

Equipment

- Four bases
- One softball

Setup

Split up athletes into equal lines at all infield positions (excluding pitcher). You should have five lines—1B, 2B, 3B, SS, and C (figure 10.3).

Execution

The ball originates at home plate. C throws to SS and then runs to the back of the SS line, following her throw. SS throws to 1B, 1B throws to 3B, 3B throws to 2B, and 2B throws to C, where you can terminate the drill or continue until every player has been to every position.

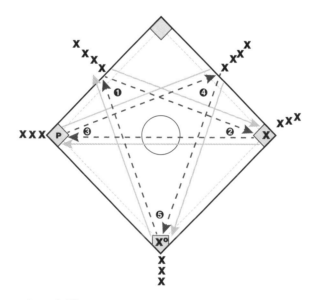

Figure 10.3   Star drill.

Next Play

Equipment
- Four bases
- One ball
- One bat

Setup
One athlete at every infield position including pitcher

Execution
Depending on your script, hit the ball to the first player and let her begin the ball movement. Potential scripts (figure 10.4 *a–d*):

1. Ground ball to P	2. Ground ball to P	3. Ground ball to P	4. Ground ball to SS
P to 1B	P to SS covering 2B	P to 3B	SS to 1B
1B to 3B	SS to 1B	3B to 2B covering 2B	1B to 3B covering 3B
3B to 2B tag	1B to 3B tag	2B to 1B	3B to 2B force
2B to C tag	3B to 2B force	1B to C tag	2B to C tag
C to SS tag	2B to C	C to SS tag	terminate, repeat
terminate, repeat	terminate, repeat	terminate, repeat	

After the pitcher fields and throws the ball, she needs to exit the field to avoid being hit by a throw.

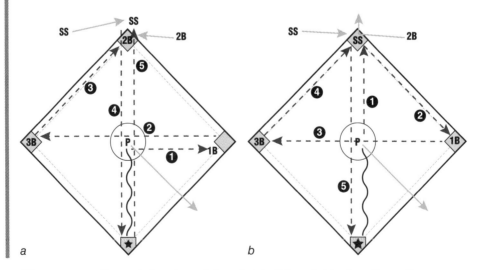

a   *b*

Figure 10.4   Potential scripts: (*a*) script 1; (*b*) script 2. *(continued)*

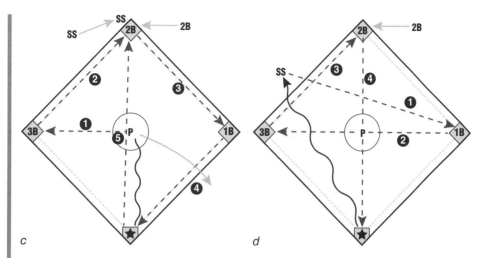

Figure 10.4 *(continued)* Potential scripts: (c) script 3; (d) script 4.

Daily Dozen

Who is the most neglected player on the field? The catcher! She catches all those bull-pens, blocks all those balls, and then is expected to throw out or pick off a runner. But how many times do you practice those throws? Once between innings is not nearly enough. Pitchers throw, and catchers call out which base they will be throwing to this set. Encourage catchers to use different targets so that your infielders stay productive and focused: Catcher A throws to 1B, catcher B throws to 3B, catcher C throws to 2B, and they then switch on the next rotation.

Equipment

- Basket of balls
- Four bases
- Catcher's equipment

Setup

Have all catchers gear up.

Execution

Each catcher gets three pitches before switching to a new catcher. Pitchers can stay through one cycle of catchers before switching. After each catcher has thrown to all three bases, she gets three more throws in which she can throw to each base or work on one in particular if she wants to focus there. Your defense gets involved in the drill deciding who is covering the base on a steal or pickoff as well as working on the footwork, positioning, and tags at every base.

Knee Throwing

Equipment
Softballs

Setup
Players begin 10 feet (3 m) away from each other with the throwing knee on the ground and the glove knee pointed toward the partner. Gloves are on the ground in front of the players so that they do not throw the ball too hard while working on flips. The throwing arm lifts to 90-degree angle with the ball in hand. Fingers should be gripped around the C of the ball to get a true flight of the ball, and players can pull down on the seams.

Execution
Players snap down on the ball trying to get a tight rotation. They rotate the body so that the glove arm is pointing at the target. The throwing arm is at a 90-degree angle behind the head in throwing position, and the ball is away from the head. Athletes then pull with the front arm down into their side. This causes rotation in the body and brings the ball to the position they were just in. They can release the ball and focus on rotation of the ball. They follow through to the ankle of the glove-side foot.

They stand up and back up to 20 to 25 feet (6 to 8 m). They do the Four-Count Throwing drill listed next, which has the athlete focus on the basic throwing technique. It is essential for beginners. It is also beneficial at the beginning of every season as you focus on the basic fundamentals of the game.

Four-Count Throwing

Equipment
Softballs

Setup
All team members are broken down into pairs.

Execution
Team members begin 15 to 20 feet (4.5 to 6 m) apart facing each other. Step 1—the athlete with the ball points the throwing-side foot at a 90-degree angle. Step 2—the athlete lifts the elbows parallel to the ground. The front arm points at the target, the back elbow points away, the elbow is bent 90 degrees, and the ball is facing away from the target. Step 3—the athlete extends the front arm and pulls back into the side. The back arm comes through the slot and releases the ball near the ear. Step 4—coming quickly after step 3, the hip comes to closed position.

Long Toss

Equipment
Gloves and softballs

Set Up
Team members are broken up into pairs

Execution
The goal of this drill is to improve arm strength and leg drive. After a proper warm up, team members are at 50-60 feet making 6-10 throws each. Once the athletes complete one set they should move back 10-15 feet, and work back to 120-150 feet depending on athletes age and the point you are in the season. Preseason should be shorter and as it progresses keep moving back. Emphasis should be put on leg drive, throws should be on an arch. As the distance increases, the arch should increase.

Catch

After the ball is thrown, someone must catch it. We talk to players early about catching the ball with two hands, and we tell them to do this to secure the ball. This is true, but as they get older and the speed of the game increases, the second hand becomes more important in helping players get rid of the ball quickly.

Receivers should give a visible and audible target. The glove should be shoulder height with a wide base. The receiver should be calling for the ball (probably not at first base, but for relays and double plays, for example). As the ball approaches, the receiver should step to the ball with her glove-side foot helping her to reach throwing position quicker. She catches the ball with two hands and moves the ball to the release point efficiently. Watch for extra arm movement or players dumping the ball from the glove rather than getting it out of the glove with the throwing hand. Flat hands training tools can help with the transition part of the drill.

Take time during practice to instruct your players to catch the ball on the throwing-hand side. After they can do that, the next step is to move the feet into a throwing position as they receive the ball. They can then make the reception part of the throwing motion so that they can get rid of the ball quicker. During your throwing program have the first basemen work on their stretch while receiving the ball. These repetitions are free, so take advantage of them. Watch your players intently during your throwing program, while they are taking ground balls, when they are throwing to bases, and when they are receiving throws from the outfield during relay drills. Make sure they are working on their catching and transferring techniques because on game day those efforts will make the difference between a runner being out and safe.

First Base

First base is an important position to round out your infield. The player in this position should have good agility and reactions and should generally be a taller athlete. She does not need to cover as much ground as a middle infielder does, but she still needs to be mobile enough to charge bunts, help on short pop flies, and close down the gap between herself and the second baseman.

Coverage

The first baseman should be in a position where she can easily drop step back to the base in three or four steps. The player should not only be able to dive to cover the line but also have enough range to close down the gap between herself and the second baseman.

In a bunt situation or with a left-handed slapper up, the first baseman typically takes a few steps toward home plate in an effort to cover the bunt. But she must be in a position where she can beat the runner back to the base.

Coverage in regular defense and bunt and slap defenses can be worked on throughout practice, and the coverage may differ between your first basemen.

Typically, the first baseman is used for relays from the outfield to home plate. On a ball hit to the outfield, the first baseman lines herself up to home plate. She first needs to know the outfielders' arm strength to decide how far out she needs to be, but generally she stands somewhere between the pitcher's mound and the baseline. The first baseman should work on this footwork while playing catch and within relay drills.

Footwork and Receiving the Ball

When the ball is put into play, the first baseman must drop step or open her hips toward the field of play to get back to first base. When she is on the base, her weight should be on the ball of the foot in contact with the base. This positioning will help prevent her from pulling her foot off the base and allow the other foot to move easily and be more mobile on throws that may take her away from the base. A common mistake of a beginner first baseman is to step too early. To correct this problem, have the first baseman practice stepping toward the ball. At the same time, she wants to make sure not to stab at the ball with her glove, but to let it come to her.

Ideally, the first baseman receives a perfect throw, but often that is not what happens. For the first baseman, the first priority is catching the ball and the second priority is the base. If a ball pulls the first baseman away from the base, she should always tag the runner, even in practice. When the ball is in the dirt, the first baseman has a few options to field the play. If she recognizes the poor throw early enough, she can create a backhand or forehand by positioning her body in a way to finish the play. A way to get first basemen comfortable doing this is to have them position themselves like first basemen instead of standing stationary when they are taking short hops. The first baseman's job is to finish the play and take pride in helping the other infielders complete routine and great plays.

Tip for receiving: Always have your first baseman start in normal position during drills. Practicing footwork to the base and stepping at the ball every time will improve her skills at the position.

Bunt Coverage

When playing regular bunt defense coverage, the first baseman should be in a few steps more than normal. On a right-handed hitter, she is the first to see the hands move, so she should communicate this to the rest of the defense. As the right-handed batter shows bunt, she should begin moving toward the bunt. As the pitch comes, she should work her way back toward the line to cover that area. This positioning helps to limit the push bunt and allows her to cover more balls that are bunted to the pitcher. If the batter pulls back and slaps, the first baseman freezes and gets into a good defensive position. She is also responsible for getting back to the base or communicating with the second baseman about who is covering the base.

On a lefty slapper, bunt coverage could look a lot different. The defense could be played with the first baseman back, who then has the responsibility to cover the base or a short swing to her side. In a regular bunt defense, she must be able to recognize the bunt or swing early. She will take more of a straight-line charge on this defense to limit the slapper dragging the ball with her down the first-base line. Also, the first baseman needs to be able to get back to the base if the slapper swings.

Pickoffs at First

The footwork back to the base on a pickoff can happen in one of two ways with the first baseman covering. First is normal footwork facing the field. This method gives the catcher a target on the inside of the base and allows the first baseman to throw quickly to second if the runner tries to advance. Against an aggressive base runner who might attempt to take second, this could be a good setup play to get her to run and attempt to get the out. The second way is to stand a little closer to the base and open up toward the foul line. This option makes the catcher's throw easier and allows the first baseman to adjust if the throw is off target in foul territory. When the player is closer to the base and opens toward the foul line, the attempt to get the runner out tends to be quicker.

Receiving

Equipment

- Bucket of balls
- Base

Setup

The first baseman starts in her ready position.

Execution

On "Go," she gets back to the base and receives a throw from a coach or player. The thrower moves around to different spots on the field and mixes in good and bad throws (figure 10.5).

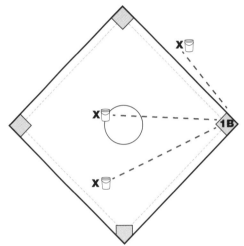

Figure 10.5   Receiving.

Bunt Coverage

Equipment

- Bucket of balls
- Base
- Receiver at first base

Setup

Lay out three softballs in positions where a first baseman would typically field a bunt.

Execution

Have the player start in ready position, charge to one ball, throw it to first, and return to ready position. She then does the same thing for the second and third softballs.

Second Base

The second baseman is typically considered to be as athletic as the shortstop but may be lacking in arm strength, so she ends up with the shorter throw to first. The only problem with this theory is that the only throw she makes that is shorter is the one to first. She is still a relay from the right fielder and turns double plays. So arm strength is a consideration, but she should still have a considerably strong arm for all her throws. She is also responsible for covering first base on bunts and pickoffs, so she must have good game instincts and be able to communicate well.

Coverage

The positioning of the second baseman is determined by the defensive play and what type of hitter is up, but primary positioning is evenly between first and second base and 15 to 20 feet (4.5 to 6 m) behind the base line. Many times the second baseman is moved in slap defense. The most we move her is even with the base line. If we are going to play an inverted defense, we move the first baseman in and over toward the circle and move the second baseman by the bag because she is going to cover a bunt. We believe that the first baseman is used to playing balls that are on her quicker and the second baseman is used to covering first in a bunt situation, so we let them stay in these roles.

Second-Base Angles

The second baseman has a wide area to cover—from the 3-4 hole to behind second base and short fly balls in the outfield to the infield blooper behind the pitcher. She must have a great first step in every direction.

Cone Drill

Equipment
- Two cones
- Bucket of balls

Setup

Have the player get to her starting position. Place a cone at a 45-degree angle on each side and 6 to 10 feet (2 to 3 m) away from the player.

Execution

Roll a ball in the direction of either cone. The player should work on getting behind the cone to field the ball as either a forehand or a backhand, or get in front of the ball if possible. Work each side in the drill. Then as you begin to hit the ball at the second baseman and take the cones away, you should see her taking these angles naturally.

Relays

Most teams use the shortstop as the primary relay person, but the second baseman has relay responsibility when the ball is hit to right field. She has to make throws to third base or home depending on where runners were to start the play. When she is the relay, she should be big and loud. She needs to be a visible target for the right fielder by having both hands up and communicating with the outfielder, letting her know in which direction she is expected to throw the ball (second base or third base). As the ball comes to her, she opens up so that she can use the momentum of the throw and redirect it to the appropriate base. We use Rocket Relay to work on the footwork and communication at every position.

Rocket Relay

Equipment

Softball

Setup

We put an outfielder on one end of the line and a catcher on the other. All potential relay people are in the center (figure 10.6). (We use multiple lines at once.)

Execution

The outfielder begins the drill by throwing the ball behind her that she retrieves and throws to the relay. The relay works on footwork and communication skills and relays the ball to the catcher, who receives and makes a tag. Going back, the catcher acts as if she is receiving a pitch and is throwing to second base on a steal. The relay moves the ball to the outfield, and we go again.

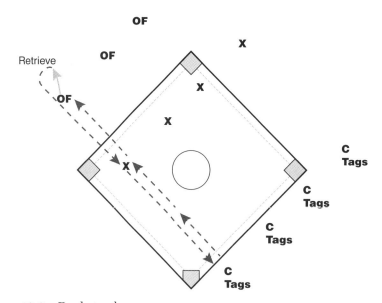

Figure 10.6   Rocket relay.

Double Plays, Throws, Footwork, and Communication

The second baseman must be adept at making several types of throws as well as performing several types of footwork at two different bases. She must be able to flip or toss the ball on the move to both first base and second base, make stationary throws from her knees to both bases, and execute the throw back to first after moving full speed toward second base. Several of these throws should be performed during the position throwing program, but it is also helpful to work in different ones daily during ground-ball work.

The footwork for a second baseman is diverse. At first base she should place her left foot on the front of the bag, shortening the throw and giving the thrower a big target. If she is quick enough, she may try to take a first baseman's stance on the bag, but we have found that she has more issues with bad throws if she worries about the stretch.

At second base her primary footwork is going to be left, right, left. Whether she is taking a throw from a shortstop coming at the bag (staying behind the bag to protect herself from a runner) or from a third baseman on the line (coming across the bag to make the throw shorter and protect herself), she should step on the bag with her left foot and secure the ball, push off with the right foot to make the throw, and step with the left to follow through on the throw. Lastly, on a play at second that she knows is going to be a force, she becomes a first baseman by placing her right foot on the bag and stretching for the ball.

Shortstop

The shortstop is often the best athlete on the field. She has the role of being one of the leaders on the infield and has to cover a lot of ground. Typically, the shortstop has a strong arm, a lot of range, and the ability to communicate well.

Coverage

Positioning for a shortstop may change depending on the player, situation, pitch call, or batter. With a left-handed slapper at the plate, the shortstop has to step up to the baseline and move over toward third to cover the gap between herself and the third baseman. In a double-play situation or with two outs, the shortstop generally plays deeper and more toward the middle so that she has more range and can turn the double play easier.

A shortstop has a clear view of the catcher's signs and should communicate this to the outfielders. With this communication, all players should have an idea of where the ball could be hit with the pitch that is thrown and know where they are going with the ball in that situation.

Shortstop Angles

As a shortstop moves to cover ground from side to side, she should take the angle that gives her the best chance to field the ball, which is back at about a 45-degree angle. Even when she dives, she should be able to see her body in this angle from her starting position. On a ball up the middle the angle could change to facilitate an attempt to cut it off. A drill that works angles, Cone Drill, is explained in the section "Second Base."

Relays

The shortstop is a relay person in many plays. When the ball is hit to the center fielder all the way to the left-field foul line, she is responsible for being the cut and lining up in a position to complete the play to a base. The relay person needs to be big and loud, putting both arms up and calling for the ball, so that the outfielder knows where to make the throw. Even on a routine base hit with no one on base, the shortstop needs to line up in correct relay position. If the ball is hit into a gap, the shortstop moves out farther to become the relay.

If the ball is hit to the right side of the field, the shortstop covers second base and communicates with the second baseman on where to line up the throw as the relay person.

Double Plays, Throws, Footwork, and Communication

Good footwork on a double-play ball allows the player to get rid of the ball as fast as possible. When receiving a ball from the pitcher or second baseman, the shortstop should position herself behind the base with the glove hand and throwing hand up. As she comes across, the throwing-side foot should drag across the back corner of the base, and the transfer of the ball to the throwing hand should happen quickly. If she is receiving a ball from the catcher or first baseman, the shortstop wants to position herself on the inside part of second base. This positioning will allow her to avoid the runner while still turning the double play. On this play, the glove-side foot hits the inside part of the base. After hitting the base, she moves her weight quickly on to her back foot to complete the throw. In all cases, making the first out is paramount on a potential double play, so the shortstop needs to recognize plays when she may have to take the throw as a first baseman would.

When the shortstop is the one making the initial play off the ground ball, she can use several techniques to transfer the ball quickly to the second baseman to speed up the double play. When moving toward the middle, the shortstop uses a flip. She should communicate to the second baseman that a flip is coming. If the ball is hit right at the right-handed shortstop, she can quickly move her weight to her right foot and use a three-quarter or side-armed throw to get rid of the ball quickly. When the shortstop is moving to her backhand side toward the 5-6 hole, she makes a full throw back to second base.

One of the most important parts of being able to turn double plays is the players knowing the situation and communicating with each other. Yelling, "Two," "Flip," "Yes, yes," or "No, no" can help the player fielding the ball know where she should be going with it and how it should get there.

Double-Play Footwork

Equipment
Softballs

Setup
Bucket of balls and coach set up behind pitchers' circle

Execution
Coach rolls ball to second baseman who starts double-play flip or throw to shortstop who is coming across the bag. Then coach rolls ball to shortstop who throws or flips to second baseman who is coming across the bag (figure 10.7).

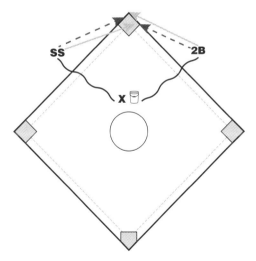

Figure 10.7   Double-play footwork.

Accelerated Runners

Another way to improve double-play time is to use accelerated runners. The runners move three to four steps up the baseline at home and first. The players then realize how quickly they have to get rid of the ball, and they get used to players running at them while turning the double play.

Equipment

- Bucket of balls
- Base runners
- Bat
- First baseman

Setup

Base runners move three to four steps up the baseline at home and first. The coach hits ground balls from home plate.

Execution

Base runners run to first and second when the ball is hit either to shortstop or to second base. The defensive players then realize how quickly they have to get rid of the ball.

Third Base

The third baseman for your team should be quick from side to side and have good reactions and no fear. This player typically has a strong arm and good instincts for the game. The third baseman has to take control in bunting situations and lock down the left side of the infield.

Coverage

The ready position of a third baseman should be the lowest of the infielders. She typically receives the ball the quickest, so she needs to be in a low squat position with her glove starting at her knees. She can then react down to a hard ground ball or protect herself on a line drive.

The third baseman typically plays in front of the base to have good coverage to the line and into the gap between her and the shortstop. She has to cover bunts, help with short pop flies, and field her position. This position changes according to the batter. If a left-handed slap hitter is up, the third baseman might move up a few steps to cover the potential bunt and allow herself to get rid of the ball quicker on a ground ball. Against a power hitter who is not a bunting threat or with two outs, she may line up behind the base to give herself more time and more range.

The third baseman may have to be in a position to cover third base on a steal as well. She needs to communicate with the shortstop about assignments, but when covering third is her responsibility, she needs to be comfortable going back to the base.

The third baseman should take ground balls from close up, from regular position, and when playing behind the base so that she is comfortable with all three depths.

Bunt Coverage

When playing regular bunt defense coverage, the third baseman should be in a few steps more than normal. On a left-handed hitter, she is the first to see the hands move, and she should communicate this to the rest of the defense. As the batter shows bunt, the third baseman should begin moving toward the bunting lanes. As the pitch comes, she works her way back toward the line to cover that area. This positioning helps to limit the push bunt and allows her to cover more of the balls that are bunted to the pitcher. If the batter pulls back and slaps, the third baseman freezes and gets into a good defensive position. If she does not field the bunt, she has to get back to third base to cover.

Against a lefty slapper, bunt coverage could look a lot different. The defense could be played with the first baseman back, so the third baseman and pitcher then have to cover all bunts. In a regular bunt defense, the third baseman must be able to recognize the bunt or swing early. By slowly approaching on a bunt until the batter commits to bunting, she will be better able to cover all types of hits.

Bunt Coverage

Equipment
- Bucket of balls
- Base
- Receivers at first base and second base

Setup
Lay out three softballs in positions where a third baseman would typically field the bunt.

Execution
Have the player start in ready position, charge to one ball, throw it to first, and return to ready position. She then does the same thing for the second and third softballs. Repeat with the player throwing to second base trying to get the lead runner.

> ### Reaction Time
>
> #### Equipment
> - Tennis balls, Lite Flites, or some other lighter ball that will not injure your player
>
> #### Setup
> Hit from home plate
>
> #### Execution
> Hit ground balls and line drives at your player. Have her take these repetitions at all three depths as well. Hit to various angles to force the third baseman to dive, field backhands, jump in the air, and protect herself.

Outfield Play

Outfield play can be broken down into several vital areas—speed, arm strength, ball recognition, angles, and aggressiveness. The first two are the easy ones. We ask outfielders to cover the most ground and make the longest throws, so speed to cover ground and arm strength to throw the ball to the plate are important. But can they get to the ball in such a way to set themselves up to make that throw? When they get there will they have the determination to make the play that is necessary?

Do you remember back in high school and college when you said, "Why do I have to learn math or geometry when I will never use it?" Well, guess what, it rears its ugly head in the outfield. Angles and acceleration are important in the outfield. Players have to judge the ball off the bat to know what angle to take and how fast to travel so that they can meet the ball at the proper point, stop it, and then change its direction and apply enough force to reach another point in time to put out an advancing runner. Translation: Get to the ball and be in proper position to throw it to the next player, who must make a tag or relay it.

Speed is a must in the outfield. Or is it? If an athlete takes the proper angle to the ball and gets a good jump, speed is a bonus, not a necessity. The outfielder's first step is the most important one because it sets the angle to the ball. The drop or open step is important. The outfielder should drop the foot and open the hips to a 45-degree angle on the side the ball is hit and gain ground so that the second step also gains ground on the ball. On a ball over her head, she should travel 4 to 6 feet (1 to 2 m), depending on size and age, from where she began. When she pursues the ball, her glove should remain tucked until she reaches for it at the last second. Many younger outfielders want to extend their arm and run, thinking the ball is going to fall into it. This technique slows them down and negates any chance of making a catch. Use tennis balls without gloves for drop step drills and then progress to gloves and game balls. Lastly, after the athlete catches the ball, she should stop immediately and turn over her glove shoulder to throw the ball.

Diving

Diving is a teachable skill, but the athlete who does not hesitate is a true outfielder. On the other hand, you have to make sure that your outfielders dive as a last-ditch effort, not just to dive. Most outfield plays can be made by running through the ball and catching it at its lowest point, but when those efforts will not get it done an outfielder has to dive. We use both the headfirst dive and a feet-first slide for our outfielders.

When attempting a headfirst dive, the athlete must remember to extend both hands as if she is diving into a pool. If she keeps the throwing hand under her, she runs the risk of injury when the weight of her body and momentum hit the ground. She should try to land more on her chest; the knees should be the last thing to hit the ground. A sliding dive allows the outfielder to pop up quickly and make a throw. This method is effective with a runner at third. The player uses a basic figure-four slide and secures the ball at about waist level. Diving can be taught inside on gym pads with athletes starting on their knees and falling forward. At full extension, they attempt to catch a ball that is tossed to them. Do forehand, backhand, and straight on. Then move to standing. They usually have to take a step and then dive. Finally, have them sprint and dive onto the mat. After they are comfortable with diving on mats, go outside. Use the same progression.

Relays

When the outfielder is deep or the ball is hit over her head, she may require a relay to get the ball to the base. She needs to understand that she is throwing the ball *through* the relay person, not to her or over her. The throw should be head high when it reaches the relay person, making her decision to cut off the ball or let it go much easier. Balls need to be lasers, not rainbows. The looping throw that gets to the plate may not be a good throw if there was no play at the plate and runners advanced behind the ball.

Backups

An outfielder should never grow roots in one spot. Just like an infielder, she should move on every pitch. If the ball is put in play, she needs to back up either the play, a potential throw, or possibly a second throw. You have to pay attention to this at practice because it will pay off in a game. Give the outfielders assignments on every play. Praise them when they back up a play that is made ahead of them. That one time when the play is not made and they are there to back up, you will be thankful. The backup should be deep enough to make a play on a deflection or overthrow. If the outfielder is too close to react to either, she might as well have stayed in her original position. Make sure to show her the proper depth in practice and the result if she is too close to the play.

Defense does not just happen. This part of the game entails repetition after repetition. Skills should be broken down and perfected, but there is nothing like a few hundred ground-ball or fly-ball repetitions to build confidence and perfect skills. Make a list of situations and practice them or at least discuss them so that your athletes are prepared to be successful when the time comes.

Chapter 11

Offensive Situational Practices

Lonni Alameda

Situational hitting is important in softball. Becoming a successful situational hitting team is not easy, but teams need to do so to compete at a high level. Simply defined, situational hitting is the ability for teams to maximize their strengths and minimize their weaknesses. Some people think that situational hitting is simply the ability to bunt a runner to second. Yes, that is part of one strategy, but it is definitely not the only component of situational hitting.

This chapter identifies four situational hitting strategies you can use as a coach. This list is not exhaustive, but it gives a good starting point. Next comes a discussion of various situational hitting strategies. The subsequent section explains how to identify personnel, or the players and athletes, on the team. Developing a specific and useful practice plan is discussed next. At this point, there is nothing left but to implement the team's strategy into games. Finally, this chapter covers how to discuss and evaluate the desired outcome of situational hitting with players.

Part 1: Four General Strategies for Teams and Players

These four strategies are the most popular ways for coaches to try to score runs with the personnel that you have on your team. Each strategy will examine both possible positive results and expected failures.

1. Home Run, Take a Hack

This strategy (table 11.1) includes teams or players who swing for the fences. The obvious goal of this strategy is to hit home runs, but from one at-bat to the next, players are trying to hit the ball in the air as much as possible. In most of their at-bats, they are trying to drive the ball to the outfield and hit either a home run or an extra-base hit. Will this happen every time? Of course not, but this is the mentality and style of swing that the players use throughout the game. As discussed throughout this chapter, greater reward (home runs or extra-base hits) brings greater risk. In this strategy, strikeouts are what we call expected failures. If a player swings big and has a high home-run total, the coach should expect a higher number of strikeouts.

Table 11.1   Strategy for Home Run, Take a Hack

Goal of strategy	Good outcomes	Expected failures	Poor outcomes
Home run Extra-base hit	Home run Extra-base hit Hit Walk	Strikeout Fly ball to outfield	Ground ball Weak out (flare)

2. Contact and Pressure the Defense

This strategy (table 11.2) is normally employed when a team or player has speed. To maximize the speed attribute, players are encouraged to put the ball on the ground as much as possible. Because ground balls are favored, players commonly use bunting and slapping as well as hitting. Ground balls have a high value because they put more pressure on a defense. Ground balls increase the number of players who must handle the ball before an out is made. This scenario increases the odds that a defensive mistake will occur, thereby creating an offensive opportunity. In this strategy, ground-ball outs are expected failures. Fly balls and strikeouts are poor outcomes

Table 11.2   Strategy for Contact and Pressure the Defense

Goal of strategy	Good outcomes	Expected failure	Poor outcomes
Put the ball in play on the ground	Hit Extra-base hit Walk	Ground-ball out	Strikeout Fly out

because they diminish the value of speed. Ask yourself this: Have you ever seen a fly ball take a bad hop?

3. Contact and Put the Ball in Play

In this strategy (table 11.3) the first and only goal is to put the ball in play as many times as possible. Players do not need to worry about how or where the ball is going, as long as it is fair. One common attribute of this style is choking up or shortening up with two strikes. Because of the value of putting the ball in play, strikeouts are considered a poor outcome of this strategy.

This strategy is best used against a dominating pitcher. A large number of strikeouts increases the confidence of the defense. You want to put the ball in play to increase the chances of finding a hole or creating an error. Increasing pressure on the defense to make a play is the goal of this strategy.

Table 11.3 Strategy for Contact and Put the Ball in Play

Goal of strategy	Good outcomes	Expected failures	Poor outcome
Put the ball in play	Hit Walk	Fair ball out of any kind (pop fly, ground out)	Strikeout

4. Get Them On, Get Them Over, Get Them In (Situational Hitting)

In this strategy (table 11.4) the goal is to get players on base, move them over to the next base, and then hit them in. Regardless of the player at-bat, this pattern is repeated. This strategy is used when a runner gets on base and the score is even or within one or two runs. Early in the game you want to try to score the first run of the game. This immediately puts pressure on the opponent. It can also be used early in the game if the team is behind by several runs but there are a number of innings to attempt to score a run or two an inning to catch up or go ahead. The goal is to get a runner into scoring position as often as possible, with the hope of scoring one run each inning. If this is the chosen strategy, all players need to be able to execute situational hitting. In this example, we define situational hitting as bunting, or the short game, hitting behind a runner, and driving in runs.

Table 11.4 Strategy for Get Them On, Get Them Over, Get Them In

Goal of strategy	Good outcome	Expected failure	Poor outcomes
Manufacture one run per inning	Getting a runner to second with two outs or preferably one out	Ball in play	Hitting in front of the runner (e.g., runner at second base, ground ball to third) Strikeout

Part 2: Identifying Personnel

Coaches can face two distinct personnel scenarios: not having control over who ends up on the team or having control. Not having control over personnel is a common scenario among high school or travel ball teams. A coach is not able to go out and pick from 40 to 60 athletes based on which players best fit the strategy. Therefore, identifying what personnel you have becomes important because the players can dictate the types of strategies used (table 11.5). In the second scenario, coaches have control over the types of players who will be on the team. This scenario is more common at the university level, at the professional level, as well as at some large-market travel ball teams. In this scenario, you can develop your strategy beforehand and recruit personnel who best fit the specific overall team strategy.

The first key to identifying personnel is to be honest with what you have. Yes, projecting where you think players should be is okay, but you have to be honest with their current skill set and what you can expect from them. The second key is to understand what strengths fit your strategy. If you want to have an aggressive, hacking team, trying to force a player with slow bat speed and a great eye into taking a hack could cause problems. To help you identify the hitters' strengths you are looking for, consult the following table. This classification is by no means definite, but it describes a general type of player who tends to fit the system well.

Table 11.5 **Strategy for Recruiting Personnel**

Strategy	Hitter strengths	Hitter weaknesses
Home run, take a hack	Power to all fields and a good idea of the strike zone, aggressive in swinging	Short game, possibly a higher strikeout player
Contact, speedy	Putting the ball in play, speed	Power or ability to drive the ball to the outfield or drive in runs
Contact and put the ball in play	Good eye, good bat control, knows the zone	Occasional power but not consistent, bat speed tends to be slower
Situational	Good eye, good bat control, ability to hit to all fields, high hitting IQ	Will give up some power in exchange for control

Note that you do not need to use only one strategy. You may decide that you need to use multiple strategies, depending on your current personnel. Most likely, your recruiting will make up a combination of all four strategies. They key is helping players understand that (1) they are different and that is okay and that (2) they will have different desired results, expected failures, and poor outcomes. For example, player A will have desired results A, expected failures A, and poor outcomes A. Most likely, all of those will be different from player B, player C, and so on. Player A should not be comparing herself with players B and C, but rather trying to be the best player she can be.

Part 3: Practice Implementation

The first piece of the puzzle in practicing situations is making sure that players understand the desired outcome of every situation (table 11.6). If they don't understand exactly what their goal is, they will not know how to execute properly. In addition, by understanding their goals, players will know when they are doing things right or wrong.

The desired outcome of each situation will change depending on the number of outs, where the runners are, the speed of the runners, the inning, the score, and so on. Here is a basic chart that will show you the desired and undesired outcomes in various situations. Note that this table it based on the situational hitting strategy. If you are using a different strategy, some situations may change. For example, a lefty slapper who is trying to pressure the defense should never be trying to hit the ball in the air.

Pitches That Will Yield a Good Outcome

After your players know the desired outcome of an at-bat, they need to learn what pitches are most likely to yield that outcome. Only certain pitches will consistently give the hitter a good opportunity to be successful based on her skills and abilities.

For example, a power hitter whose goal is to drive the ball to the outfield should likely be looking for the ball up in the zone. Few players have the ability to lift and drive a low pitch. The player needs to step up to the plate knowing that to be successful, she should be looking for the ball up in the zone. Of course, even if the player knows what pitch she is looking for, she may find it hard to lay off other pitches. She needs to practice this skill often. During front toss and batting practice, players should swing at desired pitches and let undesired pitches go.

Here is a more detailed example: A situational hitter comes to the plate with a runner at second base and no outs. From the chart, we see that a good outcome is advancing the runner to third through the short game, hitting any ground ball to the right side, a hit, or a walk. Let's assume that the goal in this instance is to hit the ball to the right side. Given all this information, right-handed hitters should be looking for the ball away and left-handed hitters should be looking for the ball inside. Therefore, early in the count, the player should not be swinging at pitches outside that zone.

Putting It Together Into a Situational Practice

One of the best ways we have found to train our players in situational hitting is to have a practice or scrimmage devoted solely to situational hitting

Table 11.6 Strategies for Practice Situations

Situation	No outs		One out		Two outs	
	Good	Bad	Good	Bad	Good	Bad
No runners	• Good contact • Barrel up the ball • At-bat of more than seven pitches regardless of outcome • Walk • Hit	• Roll over • Fisted pop-up • Strikeout	• Good contact • Barrel up the ball • At-bat of more than seven pitches regardless of outcome • Walk • Hit	• Roll over • Fisted pop-up • Strikeout	• Good contact • Barrel up the ball • At-bat of more than seven pitches regardless of outcome • Walk • Hit	• Roll over • Fisted pop-up • Strikeout
Runner on first	• Advancing the runner in any way (bunt, hit and run, slap) • Hard-hit ball • Walk • Hit	• Strikeout • Ground ball to the corners or pitcher • Fisted pop-up • Pop-up to OF not deep enough to advance runner • Not getting bunt down	• Advancing the runner in any way (bunt, hit and run, slap) • Hard-hit ball • Walk • Hit	• Strikeout • Ground ball to the corners or pitcher • Fisted pop-up • Pop-up to OF not deep enough to advance runner • Not getting bunt down	• Hard-hit ball • At-bat of more than seven pitches • Walk • Hit	• Roll over • Fisted pop-up • Strikeout
Runner on second	• Short game advancing runner to third • Any ball on ground to right side • Fly ball to RF or RCF • Hard-hit ball • Hit • Walk	• Any ball on ground to left side of infield • Pop out that does not advance runner • Fisted pop-up • Strikeout	• Any ball on ground to right side • Fly ball to RF or RCF • Hit • Walk	• Any ball on ground to left side of infield • Pop out that does not advance runner • Fisted pop-up • Strikeout	• Hard-hit ball • At-bat of more than seven pitches • Walk • Hit	• Roll over • Fisted pop-up • Strikeout

Runner on third	• Any fly ball to OF deep enough to score runner • Ground ball to middle infielders (if they are deep) • Hit • Hard-hit ball • Walk	• Strikeout • Any shallow pop-up • Ground ball to corners • Roll over	• Any fly ball to OF deep enough to score runner • Ground ball to middle infielders (if they are deep) • Hit • Hard-hit ball • Walk	• Strikeout • Any shallow pop-up • Ground ball to corners • Roll over	• Hard-hit ball • At-bat of more than seven pitches • Walk • Hit	• Roll over • Fisted pop-up • Strikeout
Runners on first and second	• Any ground ball that advances runners • Fly ball deep enough to advance runner at second or both runners • Hard-hit ball • Hit • Walk	• Any ground ball to corners • Any shallow pop-up • Strikeout • Ground ball DP or roll over	• Any ground ball that advances runners • Fly ball deep enough to advance runner at second or both runners • Hard-hit ball • Hit • Walk	• Any ground ball to corners • Any shallow pop-up • Strikeout • Ground ball DP or roll over	• Hard-hit ball • At-bat of more than seven pitches • Walk • Hit	• Roll over • Fisted pop-up • Strikeout
Runners on first and third	• Fly ball deep enough to score runner from third • Ground ball to middle infielder (runner scores) • Hard-hit ball • Walk • Hit	• Any ground ball to pitcher or corners • Shallow pop-up • Strikeout	• Fly ball deep enough to score runner • Ground ball that scores runner (no DP) • Hard-hit ball • Walk • Hit	• Any ground ball to pitcher or corners • Ground into DP • Shallow pop-up • Strikeout	• Hard-hit ball • At-bat of more than seven pitches • Walk • Hit	• Roll over • Fisted pop-up • Strikeout

(continued)

Table 11.6 *continued*

Situation	No outs		One out		Two outs	
	Good	Bad	Good	Bad	Good	Bad
Runners on second and third	• Any ball on ground (when in down angle) • Fly ball deep enough to score runner • Hard-hit ball • Hit • Walk	• Any shallow fly ball • Strikeout • Ground ball to pitcher or corners (no down angle)	• Any ball on ground (when in down angle) • Ground ball to middle infielder • Fly ball deep enough to score runner • Hard-hit ball • Hit • Walk	• Any shallow fly ball • Strikeout • Ground ball to pitcher or corner (no down angle)	• Hard-hit ball • At-bat of more than seven pitches • Walk • Hit	• Roll over • Fisted pop-up • Strikeout
Bases loaded	• Ground ball to middle infielder (must score runner) • Fly ball deep enough to score runner • Hard-hit ball • Walk • Hit	• Any ground ball to infield (not scoring runner from third) • Any shallow fly ball • Grounding into DP • Strikeout	• Ground ball to middle infielder (must score runner) • Fly ball deep enough to score runner • Hard-hit ball • Walk • Hit	• Any ground ball to infield (not scoring runner from third) • Any shallow fly ball • Grounding into DP • Strikeout	• Hard-hit ball • At-bat of more than seven pitches • Walk • Hit	• Roll over • Fisted pop-up • Strikeout

(table 11.7). In this scrimmage setting, players compete versus pitchers. Each inning has a different objective, and players strive to achieve success based on their individual or team situational strategy.

Table 11.7   Situational Practice Devoted to Hitting

Inning	Situation	Goal
1	No runners on	Get the leadoff hitter on
2	Runner at first base	Move the runner
3	Runner at second	Move the runner
4	Runner at third	Score the runner
5	Runners at first and second	Move or score the runner
6	Runners at first and third	Score the runner
7	Runner at second, down by two runs (this can change)	Add runners, avoid outs

As you can see, you can practice many situations. But depending on your strategy, players will approach each situation differently. Let's take a closer look at one inning.

Inning 5: Runners at First and Second

Home Run, Take a Hack

Hitters in this situation can still take a hack and try to drive the ball to the outfield. A runner is in scoring position, and the hitter can try to drive in this runner. Teams taking this approach are playing for a big inning in this situation. They are trying to score more than one run rather than move the runners over (possibly with a bunt) and then have two chances to score one or possibly two runs. The hitter must know that the key in this situation is to avoid a ground out to the left side. She has to wait for a pitch she can handle and either drive it to the outfield or at least hit it to the right side.

Put the Ball in Play, Pressure the Defense

A batter taking this approach would likely choose to bunt early in the count. In the worst case, the batter would be out and the runners would advance to second and third. In the best case, the batter and all runners would be safe. Although in a normal circumstance a ball on the ground to the left side would be desirable for this type of hitter, that outcome is not wanted in this situation because the defense would likely try to get the lead out at third. Therefore, lefties need to work for a ball on the inner half that they can pull on the ground to the right side or look for something to bunt.

Contact and Situational Groups

Here your hitters need to know their own strengths. Some hitters are not good bunters but have good bat control when swinging. You do not have to ask them to bunt in this situation. By practicing these situations, you and your player will learn their strengths and weaknesses. Players will build confidence in their strengths, making pressure seem less severe.

You can see from this example that it does not matter what strategy you decide to employ as a coach. What matters is that the players understand it and that you practice implementing exactly what you want. If you want to bunt or move your runners, you need to be bunting every day and practicing various ways to move runners.

Part 4: Implementing This Strategy Into Games

You have to sell out to whatever strategy you believe in. If you are going to be a certain type of team or a certain type of hitter, be that team or hitter in both practices and games. Do not expect players who have not practiced bunting during practice to be able to execute in games. Next, you must trust the strategy you have developed. You strategy may be different from that of other teams, but you have to believe in what you do. If you waver in your strategy, the players will recognize your indecision and will themselves be inconsistent and tentative. Find your identity and your path to success and stick to your beliefs. Your strategy may evolve over the course of a season, but if you are going to change, you need to work through the process again (identify personnel and implement into practice) before you can expect the execution to show up in a game.

Part 5: Identifying Desired Outcomes

We can see different strategies manifested in game outcomes through statistics. We expect to see different outcomes because teams have different strategies and personnel.

Let's first look at the final stat line of two teams who made it to the World Series in the past four years (table 11.8).

Table 11.8   World Series Stats

	Avg	R	H	2B	3B	HR	RBI	TB	Slg %	BB	HP	SO	OB%	SH
Team 1	.258	274	406	55	6	27	225	554	.353	167	60	266	.349	62
Team 2	.322	422	525	102	10	99	380	944	.578	231	36	289	.413	10

Clearly, these teams achieved a high degree of success, but as we can see from the numbers, they achieved their success in different ways. Look at the discrepancy in extra-base hits. Team 1 had 88 compared with 211 for team 2. Team 2 had a significantly higher number of RBIs and total bases and a much higher slugging percentage. Lastly, look at the discrepancy in sacrifice hits (SH). Team 1 totaled 62 on the year, whereas team 2 totaled only 10. Team 2 fits the mold of a hack, home-run strategy. They play for more than one run and clearly had success doing that. Team 1 favored the situational approach of moving the runners. They try to get someone on, bunt her over, and then work for one run in the inning. One strategy is not better than the other. Both teams had a lot of success; they simply had different personnel and used strategies that fit their personnel well.

Knowing what outcome you want is important because you need to have a way for your players to measure success. How are they going to know whether they are doing well? Something our team has started to track that does not show up in a stat line is quality at-bats (QABs). This indicator brings in more of a situational component that a traditional stat line may leave out. For example, a quality at-bat could be any of the following: advancing a runner, hit by pitch, at-bat of eight or more pitches, hard line out, fly out that moves a runner to third, and so on. This approach defines at-bats that are successful given your strategy, even when the outcome is an out.

Sometimes you may need to look at statistics for your team as a whole, and sometimes you will benefit by looking at stats of individual players. As mentioned before, if you have control over your team you may be able to recruit specific players to fit a desired strategy, but many coaches have to work with what is given to them. See table 11.9 for stats from two hitters:

Table 11.9   Stats From Two Hitters

	H	AB	Avg	XBH	Fly out	Ground out	Fly/ Gnd	Avg w/ two outs	Rnr advance w/out
Player 1	63	192	.328	10	30	57	0.5	.389	29
Player 2	74	196	.377	32	52	42	1.2	.308	9

This comparison clearly shows that these are two different types of hitters. Player 1 is a pressure-the-defense hitter. A fly ball to ground ball ratio of 1:2 would be considered average for this type of hitter. Player A has a ratio of 1:1.9. Ideally, pressure-the-defense hitters should be around 1:4; for every fly ball the player hits, she should hit four balls on the ground. In 10 at-bats, she will hit 2 fly balls and 8 ground balls. Even though this hitter's fly ball to groundball ratio is not ideal, she did have 10 extra-base hits (XBH) on the year. As mentioned at the beginning of the chapter, the tradeoff with power is usually less bat control. Someone who had fewer than 3 extra base hits would need to have a fly ball to ground ball ratio closer to 1:4.

Player 2 is a combination of a power hitter and a situational hitter. This hitter did a great job of hitting for a high average, although a true power hitter would have more extra-base hits. As expected, with more extra-base hits, the fly ball to ground ball ratio climbed to 1.2:1. An outstanding fly ball to ground ball ratio for a power hitter would be around 1.5:1.

Getting too caught up statistics can be harmful. For example, you do not want the hitter in the box thinking that to be a power hitter she needs to hit half of her balls in the air. But stats like the ones just presented offer great talking points for hitters. Use them as a way to discuss what the desired outcomes are and how well your players are achieving those outcomes.

Conclusion

You should now be able to identify various hitting strategies as well as how your specific personnel fit those strategies. From here, you should be able to develop and implement these strategies into a practice plan. After you have mastered these techniques in practice, your players should feel more comfortable executing situational hitting in games. The last piece of the puzzle is to evaluate outcomes with players and then adjust your future practices.

Remember that every player is different, so how they individually approach the game should be different as well. As athletes learn the game on a more detailed level, they will be able to maximize their strengths and minimize their weaknesses. Every player is smart and amazing in her own way. Let your players know this and help them use it to their advantage.

Chapter 12

Defensive Situational Practices

Jo Evans

I grew up in a baseball family. As a kid I sat in front of the television, watched baseball with my family, and imitated the likes of Joe Morgan, Johnny Bench, and Brooks Robinson. Baseball was my love, and I played it every chance I got, mostly in the yard, around the neighborhood, and, once in a while, on an actual baseball diamond. Reflecting back on my childhood watching baseball, in my mind's eye Morgan, Bench, and Robinson are not hitting home runs, stretching singles into doubles, or stealing bases—they are playing defense. Between the three of them, they won 31 Gold Glove Awards. When it comes to diamond sports, defense is and always will be my favorite. I love defense! I'm sure my players wish they had a dollar for every time they've heard me say, "Defense wins championships" or "You hang your hat on defense." But I repeat these expressions over and over because they are true.

This chapter includes drills, situations, scenarios, and experiences that will help you train your defensive unit to become a well-oiled machine. Breaking down a skill into smaller parts is important, repetition is important, and building confidence through hard work and persistence is important. I don't know whether any one of these things is more important than the others, but your players will follow your lead. If you pay attention to detail, they will pay attention to detail. If you demand their undivided attention, they will give you their undivided attention. If you preach, "Defense wins championships," and then prepare in daily practice for every scenario and situation that could happen in a game, your team will be prepared to prove that defense wins championships.

Identify Challenging Situations

To prepare your team for any given defensive situation or scenario, you need to identify as many different situations as possible and then practice those scenarios often enough and with pressure applied so that your team becomes comfortable executing those situations. The list of possible defensive situations is endless, but I want to focus on the situations that tend to be the most challenging for a team. Here's where I need to make one point perfectly clear. You will not have success executing any of these challenging defensive situations if you have not first spent time in practice teaching the fundamentals and mechanics of the game to each of your players. After your players can execute the basic skills of catching, throwing, fielding ground balls and fly balls, and playing defense with their feet first, then your team has a chance to excel in pressure situations and to master some of these challenging scenarios:

First-and-third situations   Bunt, lefty slapper defense

Rundowns   21 Outs

Cutoffs and relays

First and Third

The offensive team has base runners at first base and third base (figure 12.1). They can challenge the defense in several ways. They could do a straight

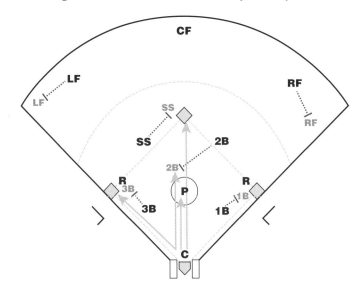

Figure 12.1   First and third setup.

steal to second base, attempt a delay steal to second base, or execute a double steal. They could attempt to steal second and intentionally create a rundown situation to distract the defense and score the runner from third base. Most of these options can advance the runner into scoring position and possibly score a run at the same time. This situation creates a lot of pressure on the defense because so many moving parts are involved.

Know Your Personnel

This defensive situation is one of the most difficult to execute. Because of the many moving parts, defensively and offensively, one slight miscue can turn the play into a disaster. The play is so difficult to defend that many teams, even teams competing at the highest levels, choose not to even attempt a defensive play. I do not share this philosophy. I believe we should train our team to initiate a play if possible. The key components to executing the first-and-third play are a catcher with a strong, accurate arm and the confidence to make an immediate throw to second base (or third) on the steal and a second baseman who can react quickly to the steal, position herself correctly behind the pitcher in a direct line with the throw, and make a quick transition with a strong throw back to the plate or to third base. Another important component is a shortstop who has a strong enough arm to make the long throw across the field to home plate. Obviously, our main goal on defense is to make sure that the runner at third does not score, but we also like to keep the runner from first base out of scoring position.

Set Up Your Team for Success

Because this play can be such a game changer, we make sure to simulate the play in practice as often as possible. We initially work on this situation without base runners. Our intention is to train our infielders on the exact mechanics of the play and the correct positioning. We want to do this in a nonthreatening environment. We want them to get comfortable and confident by going through lots of repetitions before we use base runners. Using base runners too soon can create chaos and apprehension, so it is not conducive to building confidence in your defense. Early attempts to execute the play using base runners can also make a coach crazy! After I feel confident that we understand the mechanics and positioning, we add base runners. We use our fastest and best base runners to challenge our defense. We set up this situation during our infield practice, without the outfield on defense, and have the outfielders and extra pitchers run bases.

When you initially practice this situation I suggest you do it for a set amount of time, not until you get it right. I have worn out many a middle infielder's arm because I wanted the defense to get it just right. I recommend going no longer than 15 minutes. This drill will challenge them. They won't be perfect, but drills are set up for repetition, not perfection. Most important, we set up this situation in scrimmages and live at-bats to make it as game-like as possible. We want to have a plan when running this play. One option is to anchor your first baseman on the play (figure 12.2). This setup frees up the second baseman to cheat on the steal and not be caught off guard by a fake or actual bunt. Obviously, if you are going to anchor your first baseman, you need to have a good-fielding pitcher who is comfortable fielding bunts.

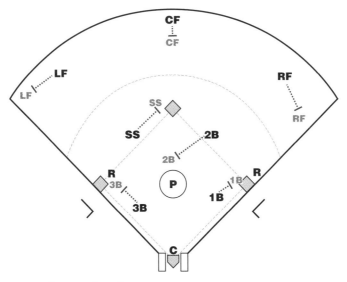

Figure 12.2   Anchoring first base.

Catcher Options

You can run many options off a first-and-third play, so make sure you know your personnel. Experiment with all your options and then settle on what works best for your team. The catcher can make a snap throw to third base to try to catch the runner off the bag. The catcher can throw directly to second base in a cut situation or all the way to the bag. The catcher can make a snap throw to the pitcher and try to catch the runner at third off the bag. Ideally, you will have several options and you can settle on which of those options are best suited to your personnel. Then make sure you practice it in realistic game-like situations. At Texas A&M we trust our catcher to read the play and adapt accordingly. Our catcher uses her instincts and doesn't worry whether Coach thinks it's the right option. It's the right option if we get an out and the runner from third doesn't score.

Rundowns

Rundowns executed poorly by a defense can be a painful thing to watch. Believe me, I've seen more than my fair share of ugly rundowns in my 30 years of head coaching. The key to being successful in rundown situations is to break down the skill, dissect the moving parts, and practice those skills individually before throwing your whole team into a rundown with runners (figure 12.3). Take the time to teach the snap throw and get your players comfortable throwing on the run. Teach them that their glove is on their hand to change the direction of the ball or redirect the ball. That transition, the skill of redirecting the ball, will come in handy in rundowns and countless other situations. Teach them that the second they get the ball, they should sprint at the runner, not trot; after the runner turns her back, she's toast. The player receiving the ball will be on the move, and the runner will have no chance.

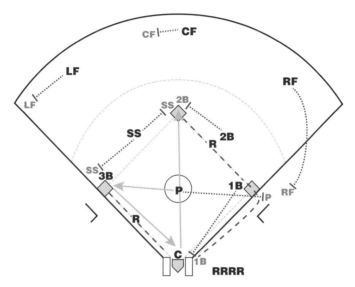

Figure 12.3   Rundowns.

One-Throw Rundown

We refer to a rundown as a one-throw rundown. We expect to make an out in a rundown situation with one throw. For that to happen, every one of our players needs to have practiced the aforementioned skills. Then we need to set up situation work in practice to learn how to execute a one-throw rundown.

We break our team into equal groups (you must have at least five players in a group) and set up two bases 60 feet (18 m) apart for each group. If you have a lot of players, you can have several groups of five spread across the field from the third-base line to right field. One person runs in the middle, and two players are at each base. We practice the skills needed to execute a one-throw rundown. After we think that everyone understands how to execute a rundown, we set up a game-like situation.

Game Simulation

We have a full defensive lineup on the field, a runner between third base and home plate, and a runner at home plate running to first base. The pitcher throws the ball to either the third baseman or the catcher to initiate a rundown with the runner between third and home. When the pitcher throws the ball to initiate the rundown at third, the base runner at home plate sprints to first base and tries to get to third base before the base runner at third gets out. After we complete the out on the base runner between third and home, our defense calls out where to throw the ball to initiate a rundown with the backside base runner. She may be between first and second base, between second and third base, or standing on third base, all depending on how quickly we get an out in the first rundown situation. I like this drill because it forces us to execute the rundown quickly and to communicate loudly where we need to throw the ball to get the backside base runner. The drill is game-like because infielders and outfielders are involved in the play, and our players have to react at game speed and make quick decisions.

Cutoffs to Home Plate

For some reason, the pitcher and first baseman often don't know when to be the cutoff on a throw from the outfield. Too often, I see players out of position in this situation. We try to keep the rules simple, but the pressure of the game sometimes gets in the way. If a play can potentially occur at first base, the first baseman stays on her bag and the pitcher becomes the cutoff person. When the ball is a line drive or a sharply hit grounder between third base and shortstop, the third baseman becomes the cut, the shortstop covers third base, and the pitcher assumes a backup position at either third or home. If the ball gets past the left fielder, the shortstop becomes the relay, the third baseman covers her bag, the pitcher assumes a backup position, and the first baseman becomes the cutoff. The catcher, of course, is an integral part of this play. She gives direction to the cutoff person so that she is in a direct line with home plate.

We initially break down the elements of this play by working what we call right side, left side. We have a full defense on the field plus an extra center fielder and an extra catcher. One coach is on the third-base side of home plate hitting to the right side of the field, and one coach is on the first-base side of home plate hitting to the left side of the field. The center fielders are positioned in left-center field for the left side and right-center field for the right side. The two center fielders are far enough apart that they are not in jeopardy of interfering in each other's play. The coaches hit balls to their respective sides, challenging them with balls in the gap, fly balls, line drives, ground balls, and so on. This setup isolates each side of the field and allows the defenders to get comfortable taking commands from the catcher and getting in a flow with the fielders on their side. After each side has become comfortable with numerous situations, we use the normal nine-player defensive alignment, place base runners, and have the coach hit to all fields.

Bunt, Lefty Slapper Defense

You have to be a little crazy to want to play a corner position in softball (figure 12.4). Our game is fast, explosive, and quick, so the ball gets on you in a split second. I shake my head at some of the third basemen and first basemen in our college game who ride that fine line of being able to cover a bunt while still being able to react to a laser shot hit right at them. The level of skill I see at the corner positions is remarkable. With the evolution of a lively ball, lively bats, and well-conditioned athletes, I find it hard to understand how someone could have the nerve to play the corners. Bunting has always been a part of the game of fastpitch. In the 1980s when I played, we were constantly bunting, moving runners, playing for that one run, and then holding on for dear life for the win. Moving runners by bunting was commonplace. Bunting is still an essential part of our game, although home runs have taken over center stage. At times, bunting seems to have become a lost art. Even so, all of us can remember times when a well-placed bunt was the difference between a win and a loss. We spend a lot of time on bunt defense. The bunting game often comes into play in the late innings when the game is on the line. Our opponent is doing everything in their power to move a runner into scoring position or squeeze a run across in the bottom of the seventh. We need to practice these situations repeatedly with pressure applied so that during a game we can handle the pressure with poise and confidence.

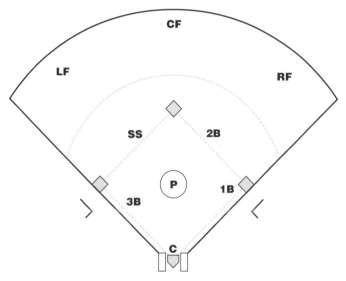

Figure 12.4   Bunt, lefty, slapper defense.

Play the Game With Your Feet

Our corners, pitchers, and catchers need to understand each other's range. Some pitchers want the ball in bunt situations, and some don't. They all need to know each other's strengths and weaknesses. The catcher has to understand each player's attributes and make decisions accordingly, in the blink of an eye. Like all the other defensive situations I have discussed, we break down, pick apart, and work rep after rep to get our fundamentals and mechanics to the point where all players are prepared to come together and execute as a team. We emphasize footwork when it comes to fielding bunts and working our bunt defense. Everything starts with moving the feet to get into a perfect position to throw to any base and to do it quickly and efficiently. We set out a cone at third base (about 2 feet [60 cm] from the baseline) and make our third baseman go around the cone to get to the ball so that she can take a direct line to first base. This drill is the most important thing we do to get our third baseman in a position to make a strong, accurate throw to first base. If she doesn't surround the ball and get her momentum going straight to first, she will likely throw a ball that tails. The first baseman will then find herself in danger of being pulled into the path of the approaching runner.

We can practice our bunt defense by having a coach toss bunts. We may have pitchers throw overhand to a coach who sacrifice bunts, slaps, and drags. We could have pitchers pitching to our outfielders as hitters, who work on their sacrifice bunts, slaps, drags, and baserunning. When we are not using runners, we use a stopwatch. We know that the quickest slappers and bunters are anywhere from 2.5 to 2.65 down the line, so we start the clock when the ball hits the bat and call out the time when the throw gets to first base. Challenging our players with the clock is an effective way to get them to play at a realistic game speed.

Anchor Play

In the college game many teams have gone to an anchor play in bunt situations. The first baseman anchors, stays back, and covers first base, and the pitcher, catcher, and third baseman field bunts. Anchoring the first baseman allows the second baseman to play up the middle and cover the steal, freeing up the shortstop to position herself for the batter and not the potential stolen base. Anchoring also allows the second baseman to shade to second base to increase the chances of turning a double play. Of course, the decision to anchor your first baseman may depend on the mobility and athleticism of your pitcher. Some teams also anchor the third baseman at times, especially if they suspect that a runner at second will attempt a steal of third base. The anchor plays are typically relayed to the corners by the coach.

Triple-Threat Hitters

Defending against a lefty slapper can be challenging, especially when that slapper runs a 2.5 to 2.6 down the line and is a triple threat. By triple threat, we mean that the hitter can drag bunt, perfectly place a ground-ball slap hit, or drive the ball in the gap or even over the wall. Olympians Natasha Watley and Caitlyn Lowe are archetypal triple-threat hitters. These hitters are nearly impossible to defend. When you play up on them to take away the bunt, they drive the ball past you, and when you play back in a normal position to have enough reaction time to field a slap hit or regular hit, they lay down a bunt.

I have seen travel ball teams run a defensive alignment in which the first baseman stays back at the bag and the second baseman moves in and positions herself between the pitcher and the first-base line. This alignment allows the first baseman to field ground balls in the 3-4 hole and cover the bag without having to turn and find the bag, essentially getting in a foot race to the bag with the lefty slapper. This defensive alignment is rarely used in the college game because of the power of the slappers, the risk of injury to a second baseman who is so close to the hitter, and the challenge that the first baseman has in getting back to the bag to receive a throw. One of the most important things we can do to prepare for slap hitters is to break down the skill of fielding the ball on the run and throwing on the run. The more our players learn to throw on the run from various positions in the infield, the more comfortable they will be on game day. Repetitions fielding the ball on the run, emphasizing proper footwork, and throwing the ball on the run are essential drills to prepare for lefty slappers. Working these situations with a stopwatch in practice will provide the game speed and feeling of pressure necessary to prepare your defense to defend against slappers.

21 Outs

A seven-inning softball game comprises 21 outs. We like to end practice with a drill called 21 Outs. You have a team on defense, and extra players run bases. The runners start at home plate, and a coach is the hitter. The coach hits the ball, and the runner runs out the hit. The entire seven innings is played with a coach as the hitter and the extra players as the base runners. When the third out of the inning is made, the bases clear and each inning starts with no runners on base. The defensive team stays on the field until they can complete 21 outs without making an error. If the defensive team makes an error, they start over at 0 outs. Throughout this chapter we have presented some challenging defensive situations. 21 Outs is a perfect drill to challenge your team with these complex defensive situations. Every even inning could be a first-and-third situation. You could start the first inning and last inning with a rundown situation. You could run bunt situations in every inning and make the third-and-first situation more challenging by running a squeeze bunt or safety squeeze bunt. The possibilities are endless.

Practice should be challenging and fun at the same time. Defense is fun. Playing great defense is a blast, but remember that your team won't play great defense until you challenge them to put in the hard work. You have to break down a skill, give your team the repetitions they need to build confidence, and train them to be persistent in their pursuit of excellence. Set the bar high. When you do, you get to "hang your hat on defense."

Chapter 13

Evaluating Practices

Donna Papa

Building a team involves developing a plan and working to execute it. Your practice plans are one of main ingredients in that blueprint. Practices have many components, and they will vary based on the coach's or program's philosophies. Three areas are important to consider with regard to practice. The first is establishing your practice foundation and environment. The process is like building a building, laying each brick with a purpose and then cementing the bricks together. My philosophy involves preparation, preparation, and more preparation. You need to settle on your philosophy and then set your standards or expectations for practice. Some of my expectations for my players every year are to be prepared, to be in the moment, to be accountable, to be positive, to be competitive, and to be on time (15 minutes early). Some of the building blocks (absolutes) of a practice plan include the development of a checklist or specifications for each area of the game. After you develop this checklist, you can them break it down to a more specific position list under each area. For example, defensive skill work could be broken down by position to include infield, outfield, catchers, and pitchers and then to specific skills such as forehands, backhands, and so on. Several areas may be included in a daily practice:

- Daily announcements and quotation of the day
- Warm-ups—dynamics, speed ladder, stretch cords

- Throwing progression
- Dailies—defensive drills
- Defensive skill work
- Baserunning
- Offensive work—hitting, bunting, slapping
- Team situational drills or competitive game situations
- Mental skills
- Vision drills
- Weights and conditioning
- Extras—team building or videos

Within each practice plan, you should specify the time you want to dedicate to that drill or situation, the players who will be involved in the drill, and the equipment and staff you need to execute the drill. You also want to identify the emphasis or goal and a standard for that drill and a potential consequence if the standard is not met.

Developing your practice plan requires time and thought. Each practice plan should have goals or objectives for each segment of it. These goals are a map to steer you in designing and molding your team. Some keys to a good practice are being productive and efficient. Most coaches have absolutes for their program in a number of areas, but to grow your program, you have to make adjustments daily, weekly, monthly, and yearly.

Weekly Blueprint

We meet as a staff on Mondays to develop a weekly plan. We have various points of emphasis for practice each week. The weekly plan involves determining what you think is important to accomplish in all areas of your program. The plan gives you a framework to use for the week. As you go through the week, you will often have to adjust your weekly plan as you work through your daily plan because you may have had to spend more time on one element of your practice than you planned. You may have to eliminate something from your daily plan and insert it the next day. Making those adjustments in the moment is okay.

Your daily plan should be specific. For each practice, you should set daily standards and expectations, establish specific time frames for each area to be covered, specify equipment setup, and communicate expectations and responsibilities of staff and managers. By honestly assessing each practice and continually evaluating and adjusting practices, you will become more successful. As a coach or staff, you cannot be afraid to change and adapt. The sooner you do the assessment after practice, the better off you will be. Looking at and talking about how effective your practice was that day will help you improve as a coach and elevate your team.

Building Blocks

In developing my program goals, I begin with the end in mind. So my starting point comes at the end of each year. An important question to ask yourself is, What do you want to accomplish in all phases of your program? I evaluate what we have done as a program overall—things we have done well and things we need to improve on. After I determine that from my perspective, I get my staff to weigh in on it. One area that always makes the list is how we run our practices and what we include in practice. More times than not, we conclude that we want to make the practices more challenging by adding more competitive elements and more consequences and accountability. I have learned that you need to be flexible when executing a practice. You may have planned an awesome practice on paper but then realize as it unfolds that a drill is not working or that you forgot to include a particular element. So as you are giving direction to players, you may change one part of what you are doing. The change may not be listed on the practice plan, but you know at that moment that it is the right thing to do. I am not afraid to make changes. You can't be so stuck on your plan that you can't tweak it on the fly if necessary. I know that many coaches post practice plans for their players, but for a number of reasons I don't do that. Posting practice plans puts you in a box with your players. If you have to make changes within the practice, they may question why. Additionally, if they are not fond of a drill, they may predispose themselves to an attitude about it. But I do share with them for each drill what our goal and standard is for that particular drill or segment of practice. You should also set time frames for each area of practice. For example, we allot 15 to 20 minutes for our warm-up, which includes a dynamic warm-up, ladder drills, and stretch cords for arm care. Following that, we spend about 10 to 15 minutes throwing and doing our dailies defensively. So I know that the first 30 to 35 minutes is devoted to warm-ups before we get into the meat of our practice.

At times I have a certain time frame planned for a drill and wind up cutting it shorter or extending it. Likewise, during a hitting drill I may realize that the activity needs a more competitive element in it, so on the second round I change it up. For example, we may be doing an angle toss hitting drill in the cage. For a right-handed hitter, we toss at an angle to simulate a curveball on the outside part of the plate. In the first round I let them hit it without any consequences. In the second round, they are out and lose reps if they pull the ball or roll it over. I wanted more accountability in the drill, so I made an adjustment that was not in my plan. You have to be willing to be flexible. You may want to use a specific drill but realize as you are doing it that the team or individual is not executing it as you had hoped, so you need to make an adjustment. Things often look better on paper than they do in the execution. As a rule, I always plan more than I need and put an extra drill in practice—a drill to use if time allows, as a backup.

Specifications

When evaluating practices, you initially need to have a plan overall and a goal for each drill. This plan can be monthly, weekly, or daily, or you can designate fall, preseason, season, and postseason. Having a plan will allow you to evaluate more effectively. For the different segments of our program—fall, preseason, season, and postseason—I ask each of my coaches for a six-week plan for each position—pitchers, hitters, slappers, catchers, and so on. Those six-week plans allow us to identify our goals and serve as our blueprint to help us achieve them. Those goals for each area allow us to develop practice plans for that time frame and for that area of our program—hitting, defense, pitching, catching, and baserunning, to name a few. We can then break that down to our weekly practice plan and then to a daily practice plan.

During the fall, we have two individual segments in which we develop our team. We are able to dictate how we divide those segments. Our team segment is usually four to five weeks, and our individual segments are usually two to three weeks before and after our team time. Within that time, we develop various plans—offensive, defensive, baserunning, and so on. For example, in developing our fall hitting plan, we had the following objectives and goals in mind:

1. Provide the blueprint for a fundamentally effective swing.
2. Use video as a teaching tool for hitters to learn.
3. Develop team offensive skills—bunt, hit and run, run and hit, moving runners, and so on.
4. Create a culture of accountability regarding ball and strike awareness.

At the end of our fall workouts, we assess each of those areas to see what we have accomplished. Based on those assessments from a team and individual perspective, we are then able to develop a plan for our individual workouts for each player. We also know where we excelled or fell short in specific areas. We believe that the coaching staff needs to get feedback from each player after both the team segment and individual segment about the areas that the player assessed as a strength and the areas that the player wanted to improve. We meet with players individually and have them fill out an evaluation sheet that we created on all areas of our program. You have to be willing to expose your program this way and be clear about expectations and what is needed to be successful going forward. This feedback is vital in evaluating what you are trying to accomplish. From these evaluations, we are able to design drills specific to players' needs. We also ask them for their favorite drills and incorporate them into the mix. Your players will be more invested if the practice or drills are specific to helping them improve.

Carolina Softball—Six-Week Hitting Plan

Goals for the Season

1. Be ACC champs by leading in runs scored, on-base percentage, slugging percentage, batting average, walks, hit by pitches.
2. Set school record for home runs with 70 or more; create a powerful offense.
3. Score 65 percent or more of our runners from third base with less than two outs; have a whatever-it-takes mentality.
4. Hit 20 points higher than our regular batting average with runners in scoring position; hit in the clutch.
5. Help each player gain an understanding of the swing and effective hitting fundamentals.
6. Build a high level of toughness and confidence in each hitter that will stand up in the big game.

Goals for Fall

1. Provide the blueprint for a fundamentally effective swing.
2. Use video effectively as a teaching tool for hitters to learn.
   - Emulation can be a great learning tool—once per week.
   - Video hitters on RVP—once per week and share that information with hitters for learning.
   - Early in fall, try to use video as an instant feedback tool (flip camera or iPad)—once per week.
3. Use exit velocity as a tool to learn about power and consistency—measure at least once per week.
4. Develop team offense skills—bunt, hit and run, run and hit, moving runners, scoring runners.
5. Create a competitive environment through simulated games, challenging drills, moving pitches, and so on.
6. Create a culture of accountability regarding ball and strike awareness.
7. Put up three signs—"Train your swing here → (arrow to the cages)," "Trust your swing here → (arrow to the field)," and "How tough are you?" on the door to the shed.

(continued)

Week 1—Individuals (45-Minute Sessions), Back to Work!

Day 1

1. Lay out expectations and goals—"Hitting is the toughest thing to do in all of sport. How tough are you?"
2. Basic drill setup in the cages—progression off tees, long tee swings, progression off front toss, feel-good front toss.

Day 2

1. Expand on attitude and start to talk a little bit about terminology.
2. Long tee drills on the field; pitch location; hop, skip, jump tee drill; step-behind drill on tee.
3. Get video on the field (RVP) and exit velocity in the cages.

Week 2—Individuals (45-Minute Sessions)

Day 1

1. Review or introduce sacrifice bunt.
2. Opposite day—all drills and front toss with opposite-field focus.
3. Adjustments—no consecutive swings with the same mistake—accountability.

Day 2

1. Mental—how to make an adjustment. What conversations are you having with yourself?
2. Review or introduce hit and run and move 'em.
3. Up-the-middle work and staying through the ball.

Week 3—Team Practice

1. Team offense—focus on sac bunting and quality at-bats.
2. Give the blueprint of the swing verbally as well as with video for support and demonstration.
   - Build from the ground up—start with the feet and finish with the hands, get into the legs.
   - Starting the swing without committing the swing by separating the front shoulder from the front hip.
   - Effectively slotting the back elbow in front of the body to stay connected.
   - Getting extension through the ball out front.

3. Use individuals before practice to show each player video and swing assessment.
4. Capture swings on video (RVP) later in the week.

Week 4—Team Offense and Opposite Week

1. Team offense—focus on hit and run, run and hit, move 'em and score 'em.
2. Emphasize staying inside the ball and driving the ball middle away.
3. Competitive attitude—challenge against the machines, curveballs away, screwballs in.
4. Thursday—start to get some feel-good swings in for game on Friday.

Week 5—Compete and Be on Time

1. Team offense—piece 3, hitter—slap, runners in scoring position, two-strike approach.
2. Be on time! How to pull the ball effectively.
3. Competitive attitude—rise or drop, and fast or slow.

Weeks 6 to 8

1. Target particular fundamental hitting areas and individual plans.
2. Team offense—compete, "Ultimate heel" offensive award.
3. Hit in the clutch—compete and get a good pitch to hit.

Adjusting Your Plan

Here is another way to look at adjusting and evaluating practice. Your preseason may be four weeks long. Based on that time frame, you may look to break it down further based on how many days you actually get to practice and what you want to accomplish during that time. As you navigate through your plan, you may have make adjustments on a daily basis because of weather or injuries or because you realize you may have to focus on one area of the game longer than you planned. During your season, you may have to focus on a certain area of the game because you need to prepare for something that your opponent does. You may be competing against an opponent whose pitcher throws a changeup to each batter in her at-bat. So you would then look to work on hitting drills that allow you to work fast or slow and drills that have your players staying in their legs when hitting. Alternatively, you may be playing a team that has a few slappers, so you would then need to work on sharpening your slap defense.

I always evaluate myself and my effectiveness with my players and staff first. I want to find out what I can do better. I challenge myself to improve in one aspect of my coaching. Additionally, I make notes and ask my staff to make notes about areas we can improve in as a staff and as a team. Here are some considerations for you to evaluate to help make adjustments:

- What is going to be most effective for the group?
- Are you confident enough to evaluate yourself so that you can get better?
- Can you leave your comfort zone to try new things?
- Can you adapt to the needs of different teams?
- Do you have an established practice philosophy?
- What priorities and principles guide you?
- How do you conduct your practices?
- What are your core values?

We also look at the areas where we were successful. As we plan for the next segment of our season, we can tweak the appropriate areas. At the end of our fall practices, for example, I evaluate what we accomplished and what I wanted to accomplish going forward in preparation for our season. I present that analysis to my staff and ask for their input. Using that information, we are able to formulate a plan to prepare for the upcoming preseason. As mentioned earlier, we also ask our players to evaluate themselves, their strengths, and the areas in which they need to improve. Their self-evaluations provide us some good insight and help us build our program, including incorporating some of their specific needs. See the attached player evaluation sheet.

From experience over a break, we know that most players spend the majority of their time hitting and fielding, not throwing. We want to make sure we start the spring in a smart way by gradually building up their arms and throwing. So our focus will be on quality and quantity of defensive reps versus a lot of throwing combined with reps. We can gradually build toward that. Being flexible and looking for new ways to do things are important.

Each team is different and brings different challenges. Coach Hutchins at Michigan uses years to name her teams—Team 29, Team 30. Team 29 is different from Team 30 and has different personnel, needs, and challenges. What works with one team may not work with another. You can maintain your core values and your absolutes, but you may have to change how you run your bunt defense or cuts and relays based on how athletic your pitcher is or how skilled your infield is.

You will have absolutes that guide your program. In addition, you and your staff will need to identify specific areas of your program that you want your team or individual players to achieve. An example of my notes is shown here. That first thing listed in my notes for the team is building trust. We have focused on that area from day 1 in our program, and we want to continue to weave it into our day-to-day culture. We know that to be successful, teams need to have a high level of trust. So as a staff, trust will be at the top of our list to promote daily. As a team, we identified what trust means, and we continue to hammer that home. We may also use video to help us hit some main points.

Lists are helpful in identifying areas you would like to focus on as a team. I created a list after our 2013 season to help guide us going forward for our 2014 fall and spring. Evaluating and looking to make adjustments right after your season allows you to keep information fresh from your most recent season. My list included 20 areas that I wanted to focus on. For purposes of this chapter, below are 6 of them.

Carolina Softball—Ideas for Fall 2014

1. Fit and fast motto—strength and conditioning.
2. Toughness book as summer read—groups of three present chapters. Use as mental piece—trust.
3. Hold the rope as a potential theme—emphasis on teamwork.
4. Go to a field hockey or soccer practice in the fall.
5. Create a quality at-bat leaderboard for the team room.
6. Reward behaviors we want to see repeated—Dean Smith, weekly stickers for helmets, what does pride, passion, and excellence look like?

After you complete your practice, you must determine whether you achieved your objectives for that day. What drills worked? What drills were not executed well? Why? Was the drill or practice too long? Was the drill clearly communicated? Did it need to be broken down more? Was it competitive enough? Did the drill challenge the players?

Grading Your Program

Your practice is your classroom. You need to establish how you evaluate your practice and how you can adjust it. How will you grade your practice at the end of each day? You need to do this constantly so that you can achieve your objectives. Additionally, you should get your athletes' feedback on a drill or some segments of practices. For evaluation purposes, shooting video of some parts of practice is helpful. You may not always see everything happening as it happens. With more time, you may be able to see something in the video that can help a player and ultimately the team. One of the best examples is filming baserunning in practice, specifically your players' leadoffs from bases.

A method we have used in our program is a report card (table 13.1) for our players and our team. We have done it for each player and for the team with regard to quality at-bats (QABs), which highlight our overall successes offensively. We got this idea from the University of Michigan because they do it for their players and their program. Here is a statistically oriented report card. You could also do one to reflect your players' toughness, effort, and so on. You determine the standards you want to use and the grade associated with each standard or area.

Table 13.1   UNC Softball Report Card

	Games 1–12	Games 13–24	Current total	ACC play
QAB %				
OB %				
Slugging %				
RISP %				
RBIs				
Runs scored				
Batting avg.				
Adv. runners				
Fielding %				
Grade:				

From National Fastpitch Coaches Association, 2016, Practice perfect softball (Champaign, IL: Human Kinetics).

We constantly evaluate our program and try to do one more thing or do something a different or better way. For example, we incorporate a defensive challenge at the end of our practice on a daily basis. We have a Tar Heel Challenge jar with numbered challenges on pieces of paper, and we then pick two defensive teams. A player from each team picks a challenge out of the jar. Both defensive teams execute the same challenge. We put a point value on getting the lead out (2 points) and getting outs in general (1 point for each out). We want to emphasize execution and being aggressive defensively. The winner of the defensive challenge is the team with most points.

Practice and practice planning are your business plan and the roadmap to the success of your program. Devote energy up front to developing your blueprint. Be detailed about your priorities, time lines, and content. Developing this blueprint will help you be more specific in breaking down each practice into the components that will allow you to achieve your goals. Identifying those components is the key to making daily, weekly, and monthly adjustments. Constantly tweaking the areas that your team or players need to be better in will help you and your players achieve their goals.

My final practice thought is summed up in this quotation: "When our works supersede our words, greatness awaits."

Chapter 14

Practicing Indoors

Jen McIntyre

If I have learned one thing after spending most of my playing and coaching career in the snowbound states, it is that nothing screams spring softball like indoor practice. I have heard it used against us on the recruiting trail several times over the years, but as we all know, it rains everywhere across the country. We have all experienced it—the gray days, cold nights, tight quarters, and limited space. So what do you do? How do you manage an entire team inside for a couple of hours? Our philosophy is to do the same mechanics inside that we do outside. We emphasize a ton of footwork and fast-feet drills inside that we can incorporate into the defense, especially with outfielders. The more we are limited by space, the more creative we can get with our indoor practices.

Assessing the Challenges and Scouting Your Resources

You need to consider several variables that will help you design and manage your practice structure indoors.

- Gym floor versus Astroturf versus rubber pellet turf
- Ceiling height versus lights
- Tennis balls versus regular balls versus Incrediballs
- Basketball gym court versus indoor football turf field

As you begin to assess your practice space, you can determine the way you will structure your defense, offense, and pitching. The infielders and outfielders experience their own challenges, yet we counterattack those challenges with several drills. The most notable difference infielders will see will be the speed of the ball. Inside, the ball typically gets to the defender much quicker because the dirt acts as an inhibitor. We counteract this by having the infielders take their starting positions behind flat cones and focus on charging the ball. We have the coach hit slow rollers so that the infielders work on attacking the ball. The outfielders' biggest challenge is that they do not get to experience the effect of wind or fly balls in the sun. We counteract this by using a string of overhead lights and hitting or throwing fly balls directly down the string of lights to get the players accustomed to using their gloves or moving their feet to get in a better position to see the ball.

Cone Drills

As we begin practice, we run and stretch as normal and then go right into our throwing progression. We emphasize footwork and receiving skills. We do a lot of around-the-horn throws, adding transitions and tags at the bases. From this point, we go into the agility portion of practice. We get creative here and get a lot out of our indoor space. We use flat cones for many footwork drills. You can emphasize drop steps, charge and throws, and change of direction in this part of your practice. The following drills are some of my favorite ones using cones (table 14.1).

Table 14.1   Cone Drills

Drill name	Equipment	Focus
Four Diamond Cones	Flat cones	Speed, change of direction
Drop Step Z Drill	Flat cones	Drop steps, hip action, acceleration
Triangle Drill	Flat cones	Change of direction, incorporating angles to the ball

Four Diamond Cones

Setup

1. Place four cones in the shape of a diamond.
2. Place one defender inside the diamond with her glove on. The cones, placed at twelve o'clock, three o'clock, six o'clock, and nine o'clock, are five yards (meters) away from the center point.

Execution

1. The defender runs in place in an athletic stance. When the coach points in a direction, the player moves to the respective cone.
2. When she retreats to the cone behind her, she must use the drop step.
3. The cone in front of her is a do-or-die grounder. The side cones are a forehand and a backhand.

Coaching Point

- When doing this drill, the athlete is shadowing each move; no ball is being tossed or rolled.

Drop Step Z Drill

Setup

This drill uses cones placed in a staggered formation approximately 5 yards (meters) apart (figure 14.1).

Execution

1. The defenders line up at the first cone, drop step to the next cone, turn and drop step to the next cone, and so on.
2. When they get to the last cone, they must sprint back to the top.

Coaching Point

This provides a good conditioning element as well.

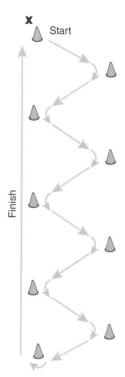

Figure 14.1   Drop step Z drill.

Triangle Drill

Setup

Place cone B 10 yards (meters) in front of the start line (cone A). Place cone C about 10 yards laterally from cone B (figure 14.2).

Execution

1. The defender starts at cone A and sprints forward 10 yards to cone B.
2. After she gets to cone B, she immediately transitions into a slide shuffle to cone C, where she does a drop step to receive a ground ball rolled from the coach.
3. You can reverse this drill to work on the drop step for the opposite side.

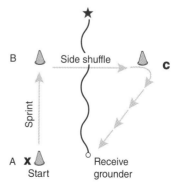

Figure 14.2   Triangle drill.

Coaching Point

This drill is a good way to incorporate the forward attack movement, lateral change of direction, and drop step to increase range. Depending on how many players you have, it can also be an effective conditioning drill.

Agility Ladder Drills

Now we are just getting warmed up. If I could recommend one item for every program to purchase, it would be an agility ladder. We use these almost every day and see a dramatic increase in foot speed and agility on defense. As the players are going through the following drills, make sure that they wear their gloves. We incorporate this drill right into the defense and have them field grounders and flies after going through the ladders. I could write an entire book about our ladder drills, but here are a few of my favorites (table 14.2):

Table 14.2 Ladder Drills

Drill name	Equipment	Focus
Two Feet in Sideways	One agility ladder, balls	Quick feet, move arms with glove
Vertical Ladder Throw on the Run	Two agility ladders, bases, balls, full team	Acceleration, throws on the run, tag plays, and force plays
Drop Step Ladder Z Drill	Two agility ladders	Quick feet, fitness, hip action, and acceleration
No False Steps	One agility ladder, balls	Acceleration forward, first step to the ball

Two Feet in Sideways

Equipment
- One agility ladder
- Balls

Setup
Place the ladder horizontally in the base path with cones as shown in figure 14.3.

Execution
1. Athletes run sideways through the ladder.
2. They then drop step inside the cone into ground balls or fly balls.

Coaching Points
Players should stay light on their feet and drive their elbows back as they run.

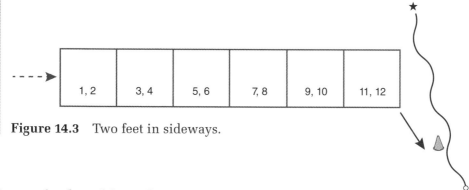

Figure 14.3 Two feet in sideways.

Vertical Ladder Throw on the Run

Equipment
- Two agility ladders
- Bases
- Balls
- Full team

Setup
Place the ladders vertically toward home plate as shown in figure 14.4.

Execution
1. The coach sits with a bucket of balls at the pitcher's mound.
2. Player 1 runs through the ladder and picks up a rolled ball to throw on the run for a force out to player 3 at first base.
3. Player 2 runs through the ladder, picks up the second rolled ball from the coach, and throws to home plate for a tag play.
4. Players rotate in a circle after every play.

Coaching Point
Focus on acceleration, throws on the run, tag plays, and force plays, alternating at the bases.

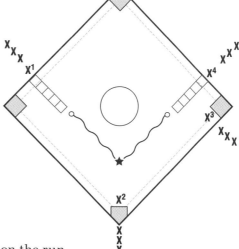

Figure 14.4 Vertical ladder throw on the run.

Drop Step Ladder Z Drill

Equipment
Two agility ladders

Setup
Place cones on a diagonal approximately six long drop steps or paces apart.

Execution
1. Player 1 begins and starts on the drop step to the next cone. She opens up on a drop step, changes direction to the next cone, and so on.
2. The second player begins after the first player reaches the second cone.
3. When the player reaches the final cone, she sprints back to the starting cone.

Coaching Point
Players should have quick feet and focus on acceleration.

No False Steps

Equipment
- One agility ladder
- Balls

Setup
Place one ladder horizontally in the base path. The coach is near the mound with a bucket of balls.

Execution
1. Players run sideways through the ladder.
2. As soon as the ball is rolled, the player sprints forward to the ball for a clean pickup without stepping backward first.

Coaching Point
Players should accelerate out of the ladder, pick up speed, and attack the ball.

Everydays

At this point, the team is warmed up and fired up. We usually then split the team into position play (infielders, outfielders, and catchers) to do what we call everydays, the drills specific to their positions for glove work, tracking the ball, and so on. We begin most of these drills with a tennis ball that they catch with their bare hands. Catching barehanded is more difficult. It requires soft hands when receiving and emphasizes tracking the ball all the way into the glove hand. We then progress to using gloves with a regular ball.

Infielder Everydays

Coaches can incorporate drills of their choice for each position. We typically do those that involve short-hop glove work, drop-step catches, double-play footwork, exchanges at the bags, back-at-an-angle plays, and so on. I recommend creating a set routine so that the players become familiar with your daily fundamentals.

Outfielder Everydays

We use this time to focus on fundamentals specific to this position. Our routine typically includes drop-step catches over each shoulder, wrong-way footwork or change of direction, Willie Mays catches directly overhead, line-drive tracking drills, and three-step drops to get behind fly balls. Again, develop a set routine for your outfielders that stresses the fundamentals every day.

Catcher Everydays

Your catchers need to do defensive position work as well. Neglecting this important work is easy, because catchers are needed to catch their pitchers' workouts. But catchers need time to learn the defensive fundamentals of the position. Framing, receiving, shifting and blocking, and transitions are all important skills that we attack during this time in practice.

One of the biggest aspects of our practices is that we compete and have fun. You can do several indoor drills to accomplish both of those tasks (table 14.3). We play a lot of Wall Ball. You can do this with tennis balls or indoor softie balls. This drill is great for working on footwork and drop steps, and it fosters competition.

Table 14.3   Catcher Drills

Drill name	Equipment and personnel	Focus
Outfielder Wall Ball	Tennis balls	Change of direction, drop steps, competition, eye–hand coordination
Infielder Wall Ball	Incrediballs or indoor balls	Charging the ball, playing the hop, sharp angles to the spot
Popcorn Drill	Four cones, two players at a time, one bucket of balls	Communication, competition, diving

Outfielder Wall Ball

Equipment

Tennis balls or indoor Incrediballs

Setup

- Place a single-file line of outfielders approximately 10 feet (3 m) from the wall.
- The coach stands only 5 feet (1.5 m) from the wall.

Execution

1. One athlete begins at a time.
2. The coach throws the ball high on the wall so that when it bounces off, the player has to drop step over her shoulder to catch it (figure 14.5).
3. The next player then takes her turn.

Coaching Points

- You can mix in wrong-way footwork in this drill as well.
- You can go as slow or as fast as you like.
- We incorporate knockout into this drill just as you would in basketball. If the player doesn't catch it clean, she is out.

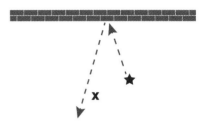

Figure 14.5 Outfielder wall ball.

Infielder Wall Ball

Equipment

Tennis balls or indoor Incrediballs

Setup

Infielders line up along the length of the gym floor approximately 15 feet (4.5 m) apart.

Execution

1. Players throw the ball as a grounder on the run and diagonally to the next player as it moves all the way down the line (figure 14.6).
2. The players must field the ball cleanly on fewer than two bounces within the boundaries or they are out.

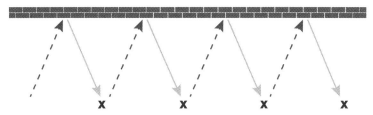

Figure 14.6   Infielder wall ball.

Coaching Points

We borrowed this drill from Patty Gasso at the University of Oklahoma and modified it a bit for our indoor space. This drill works on footwork, transitions, and picking the right bounce to field the ball. The drill can also be played as knockout, going either on the diagonal or one at a time.

Popcorn Drill

One of our favorite indoor drills is called Popcorn. This drill targets communication, change of direction, and competition. The players compete against each other to see who can catch the most balls. The drill produces game-like situations and works on communication.

Equipment

Bucket of regular softballs, four cones

Setup

1. Put the team into pairs.
2. Put four cones out on the turf or gym floor in the shape of a diamond.
3. Spread the cones about 15 yards (meters) apart, adjusting for space or skill level.

Execution

1. The coach has a bucket of balls and tosses them in rapid succession.
2. We like to do 12 to 15 fast reps and then switch to the next pair.

Coaching Points

Allow players to strategize how they are going to cover the entire diamond. Emphasize communication and aggressive play.

Strengthening Drills

One of the areas that we believe our players can improve on is strengthening their core and leg drive. We do several leg drive drills, especially with our outfielders, that emphasize lower-half explosion and throwing accuracy. One of my favorite drills for this is one we call Single-Leg Drives.

Single-Leg Drives

Setup

All the outfielders line up on the foul line.

Execution

1. They balance on the left leg (if they are right-handed throwers) with the knee slightly bent and their gloves on the ground as if they are fielding a do-or-die ground ball.

2. Have them hold this position for three seconds. When you call, "Drive," they shadow through their throw for power and strength.

Coaching Points

Emphasize covering some ground as the players are attacking in the direction in which they are throwing.

Range Fielding

This drill incorporates many aspects for your team. We have the entire team do this drill to work on taking good angles to the ball, foot speed, and conditioning.

Equipment

- Two buckets of balls
- Infield bases
- Two bats for fungo

Setup

1. You need two coaches to hit ground balls for this drill.

2. Place one coach at home plate and the other at second base.

3. Split the team evenly in half at first base and third base (figure 14.7).

Execution

1. To work on forehands first, the player at third base fields a ground ball hit toward shortstop from the coach at home plate. At the same time, the coach at second base hits a ground ball to the first player in line at first base, headed toward home plate.

2. The defenders work on going back at an angle to increase their range and foot speed.

3. The player fields the ball, simply hands it to the coach in front of her, and then continues to jog to the end of the next line. They will appear to be running in a large circle.

4. After several reps, reverse the direction to incorporate backhand plays.

Coaching Points

Emphasize going back at an angle when necessary to increase range and first steps to the ball. This drill helps athletes move their feet and take their shoulders with them when moving laterally.

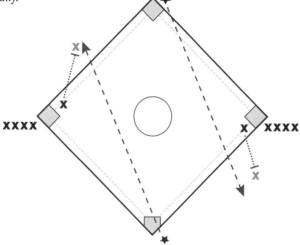

Figure 14.7 Range fielding.

As you start to put the whole defense together, your ability to do team defensive set plays will be dictated by your available space. We do a lot of bunt defense and short game or slapper sets when we are in our smallest spaces. Your infielders can also do a lot of work on your first-and-third defensive plays, squeeze defense, and infield situations. If you have enough space, you should work on communication plays as well. We like to break the field into triangle plays or in-between plays. We work on both grounders and fly balls between the following sets:

1. 3B, SS, LF
2. SS, CF, LF
3. SS, CF, 2B
4. 2B, CF, RF
5. 2B, 1B, RF
6. 3B, P, C
7. 1B, P, C

When working your outfielders into your team defensive sets, one field will be too short for distance throws in many buildings. To counteract this, we have two positions (center field and left field) play at regular depth, throw to bases, and field from there. We then simply reorient the field to accommodate center field (figure 14.8a) and right field (figure 14.8b) by moving home plate to the first-base area.

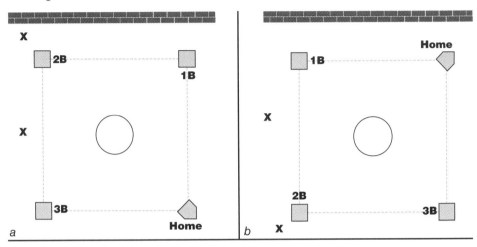

Figure 14.8 (a) Centerfield; (b) right field.

Overcoming Potential Equipment Challenges

Offensively, being indoors can pose many challenges if you do not have batting cages available. Does this mean that you cannot get your work in? Of course not; you just need to be more creative in how you manage the drills. Some facilities will require you to use indoor balls. Although we would all rather hit a regulation ball, we can still get the job done.

One item that you will absolutely need to invest in is sock nets. You can purchase four nets and place hitters on tees hitting into each side of the net. If the hitters alternate, you can have eight hitters swinging at once. When working on strengthening drills offensively, you can use deflated basketballs, soccer balls, and volleyballs because the flight of the ball will be restricted.

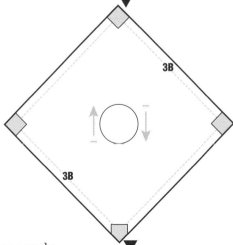

Figure 14.9 Pitchers throwing simultaneously.

If your space is limited and you would like to work on bunting, you need only the size of an infield. You can get two pitchers throwing at once, one in the direction of home plate and the other slightly to her side throwing toward second base (figure 14.9). You will have one bunter at home and one bunter at second. You can choose to have a defensive third baseman playing her position as well so that she can work on fielding bunts in front of her.

Offensive Drills

As with everything we do defensively, we like to compete in our offensive drills as well. One of those competition games is called Last Man Standing (table 14.4). Depending on the offensive focus that day, we work on bunting, opposite-field hitting, two-strike hitting, hit and runs, and other skills.

Table 14.4   Offensive Drills

Drill name	Personnel	Focus
Last Man Standing	Pitcher, catcher, bunter (full team)	Determine the offensive focus and knock out the offensive team based on the selected skill

Last Man Standing

Setup

You need only a pitcher, catcher, and bunter for this drill.

Execution

- We have the whole team participate. Each player receives only one strike to get her bunt down.
- If she executes successfully, she goes to the end of the line. If she is unsuccessful, she is out.
- The line continues until only one player is left.

Coaching Point

As players are knocked out, you can incorporate fitness into this portion (i.e., sit-ups, planks, burpees) until the last man is left standing.

Baserunning is another area that you can improve while working in an indoor setting. I have learned over the years that you don't need to be the fastest team to steal bases or score runs. If you have smart base runners and work on perfecting this skill, your run production will increase without your having to rely on base hits to get it done. One of my favorite baserunning drills is Leads and Reads (table 14.5).

Table 14.5 Leads and Reads

Drill name	Equipment and personnel	Focus
Leads and Reads	Groups of three, full set of bases	Fitness, cuts out of the box, leads and reads at the bases, sliding

Leads and Reads

Equipment
- Groups of three
- Full set of bases

Setup
Put your team in groups of three at home plate. Players go one at a time, taking a dry swing at the plate.

Execution
1. The next baserunner goes approximately when the previous player is halfway down the first-base line.
2. The first player runs out a triple to third base, the second player slides into second on a double, and the final player hits a single and runs through first base.
3. The first group of players stays at their respective bases as the next group of three lines up at home plate.
4. A pitcher goes through her motion so that the base runners can work off a lead.
5. The group at the plate proceeds in the same manner as the first group.
6. The group on the bases goes as follows:
    i. The runner at first base goes to third base and slides into the base.
    ii. The runner at second base sees a fake hit through and slides into home.
    iii. The runner at third base tags on a fake fly ball to left and then heads home.
7. When the players get back to home plate, they reorganize in their respective groups so that they run to all the bases.

Coaching Point
This drill works on leads and reads at the bases as well as conditioning.

As you can see, life in a snowbound state can be challenging, but with the right mind-set and an arsenal of drills, you can accomplish almost all the things inside that you can do outside. You should always seek new drills and find ways to keep practice moving and exciting, regardless of your space. By focusing on fundamentals, maintaining a competitive environment, and attending to the details, you will be ready to go when you can finally put away your snow shovels and umbrellas.

Appendix

Sample Practice Plans

Julie Lenhart

Suny Courtland Practice Plan

Practice Outline

4:00   Dynamic stretch
        Warm-up (sprints and baserunning)

4:20   Throwing progression and everydays

4:40   Hitting warm-up/dry swings
        Split team in half

4:50   Half of team hits—four-corner Wiffles
        Half of team does agilities—station work
        30 minutes, then switch

Agilities

Go through twice with rest between
40 seconds of work, 20 seconds off

1. Sprint, shuffle, sprint
2. One-foot ladder sprint breakdown
3. Diagonal bounds
4. Shuttle sprint
5. Two-feet lateral ladder with shuffle
6. Fast feet, directional sprint
7. Icky shuffle ladder sprint breakdown
8. Four-corner first step

Four-Corner Wiffles

Half of group hits, half of group shags balls or pitches
Each rotation is two "laps"
Four hitters form a 40- to 50-foot (12- to 15-m) square
Four tossers face them from inside the square

1. R1: three swings per base = go to next base
2. R2: three swings per base = B1: out, B2: in
3. B3: up, B4: down
4. R3: Each hitter gets one swing—to rip it or run

Rachel Hanson

Stanford Practice Plan

Stanford Softball 2014-15

Equipment: Softballs, baseballs, jbands, cones, nets for offense, tees		
Time	**Drills and Stations**	**Description/Action**
2:00	1) Dynamic warm up	
2:10	2) Band work/arm care	
2:15	3) Arm warm-up	
2:25	4) Accuracy test	Accuracy from a variety of distances (60', 70', 90')
		Partner up, 10 throws at a specified distance, how many can you throw between the shoulders and hips?
2:30	5) PPFs day number 1	
2:35	6) 4 corners	Players divide up evenly at 4 bases
		Softball starts at home - throws follow a pattern, after the throw, run to the next base
		Throw pattern - Home-2nd-1st-3rd-2nd-Home
		Tag plays at 2nd, 3rd and home, force play at first
		Time it from start to finish, team always works to beat their time
2:40	7) Split work	Middles: Double play footwork
		Corners: Back hands
		Pitchers/Catchers: Pass balls
		Outfield: Balls at the fence
2:55	8) 1st and 3rds	Review of our scheme and calls, with live runners
3:05	9) Pick-me-up drill with situations	Live runners, full defense
		Work through all possible runner scenarios (R3, R3 & R2, Bases loaded, R2, etc) - 8 in total
		Defense has to make 8 clean plays in a row. If they do, they get extra defensive reps between rounds (typically 3-5)
		After an error, they get one "pick me up" per round. They call out a teammate who then has to execute the play.
		If the teammate succeeds, they still have the opportunity to complete 8 in a row. If not, we continue until 8, with no free reps.
3:25	10) Tee warm-up, swing check-in	

(continued)

Stanford Softball 2014-15 *(continued)*

Equipment: Softballs, baseballs, jbands, cones, nets for offense, tees		
Time	**Drills and Stations**	**Description/Action**
3:35	11) Offense	Groups of 2
		Rotation: On deck, live, video review, stand-in on pitcher in bullpen, shag, shag, tee work, player front toss, player front toss
		Live: Working on counts - 0-0, 3-1, 1-2
4:20	12) Bunt competition	Outfield vs infield
		Outfield is running and practicing all/only short game: quick bunts, slapping, push bunts, drags
		Infield is on defense
		Scoring for defense: 2 points for getting the lead runner, 2 points for a caught stealing
		Scoring for offense: 2 points for safe at first and second, 1 point for safe at second/out at first, 1 point for a stolen base
		First to 10 wins

Beverly Smith

South Carolina Practice Plan

2:00   Dynamic warm-up, stretch cord routine, throw
Pitcher's long toss
Extra time, athletes begin everydays

2:30   Infield and outfield split

Infield and Outfield Split

Infield	Outfield	Bullpen light workout—60 pitches
Everydays	Everydays	Nickie, EF
Crossfire	Machine drills	Julie, MW
Daily focus	Daily focus	

3:00   Hit warm-up in cages.

Team divides into four groups for front-toss warm-up before going live.

3:15   Live at-bats, defense, pitching, and baserunning

Team is divided into four groups.

1. Group 1—live hitters and base runners
2. Group 2—team in cage
   Cage 1:   Three-plate machine
   Cage 2:   Three-plate front toss (coach)
   Cage 3:   Location front toss (coach)
   Cage 4:   Rounds on machine 2
3. Group 3—on defense
4. Group 4—on defense

Teams 1 and 2 switch and then rotate to defense. Teams 3 and 4 move to offense.

Live Situations

1. Runner at first, sacrifice—defense plays live. This is a fastball from the pitcher; the batter has an opportunity to sacrifice on the first strike. For work on bunt defense, the catcher rolls out a ball on foul balls; this moves quickly.
2. Runner at first, 0-0 count
3. Runner at second, 1-1 count
4. Runner at third, 2-2 count

Points of Emphasis

- These are live situations. Everything should be played at game speed.
- Pitchers rotate and throw to each of the four teams; each hitter gets three live at-bats.
- Specific situations are chosen to provide the defense repetitions.
- Specific situations are chosen to give runners baserunning repetitions as well.
- This is great defense and baserunning work to video and review the next day with team.
- Hitters are charted to determine the number of quality at-bats.
- Pitchers are charted to determine spot percentages.
- Coaches can give signals to hitters and base runners to keep defense honest.

5:00 You make the call (quick review of a game rule; describe situation and call on a player randomly for answer).

Rachel Lawson

Kentucky Practice Plan

Round 1: Warm-up
- Dynamic Warm-up
- Throw long

Round 2: Relay Mechanics
- Four team relay race in lines

Round 3: Isolated Fundamentals
Outfielders
- Put a ball in the glove – run and dive with the ball in the glove and get up quickly to make a throw to a stationary cut position.

Infielders and Pitchers = Double play and Diving Circuit
- Catcher, 3rd baseman and 1st baseman – put a ball in the glove, dive and quickly get up and throw home.
- Pitcher, 2nd baseman and shortstop – the pitcher, SS and 2nd baseman are live. They will receive a ground ball and fielder in charge of covering the base will turn a double play to 1st *(there will be a stationary receiver catching balls at 1st and placing them in the bucket).*

Round 4: Isolated Fundamentals
Outfielders
- Coming through the catch – long hops home

Infielders
- 3rd baseman, 1st baseman – starting position behind the base. Receive a ground ball and finish the play at 1st.
- Shortstop and 2nd baseman – start with a ball in the glove, dive up the middle and then get up quickly and make a throw home.

Round 5: Isolated Fundamentals
Outfielders
- Field line drives in position – the hitter's focus is on hitting line drives.

Infielders and Pitchers
- Communication balls – 3rd baseman and shortstop: the ground ball is hit in the 5/6 hole. Both fielders communicate who will be fielding the ground ball. The other fielder will break to cover their base.

- Communication balls – P, 2nd baseman and 1st baseman: ground ball is hit between 2nd, 1st and the pitcher. Communicate who will field the ground ball and either 2nd or 1st release to cover 1st base.
- Catcher: comes out of the squat to field a bunt and then throws to 2nd *(stationary fielder at 2nd)*.

Round 6: Isolated Fundamentals

Outfielders

- Live balls in position

Infielders and Pitchers

- 1st and 3rd defense using ghost runners

Round 7: Team Base Running - Isolated

Lead Races (play what you see) – live pitcher, catcher and fielders:

- 2 lines of runners at 1st (isolated):
  - Ball in the dirt = run to 2nd
  - If the catcher makes a move to pick-off = dive back.
- 2 lines of runners at 2nd (situation is 2 outs, 2 strikes on the batter)
  - Read the pitch – if it appears to be a pitcher that the hitter must attack with 2 strikes, take off for 3rd.

Round 8: Team Base Running - Situational

- Runner at 2nd and a hitter running at the plate – live defense, coach will fungo from the plate. The base runners react to the depth and distance of the hit. The defense must finish the play focusing also on trail runner defense.

Round 9: Team Base Running - Situational

- Runner at 1st and a hitter running at the plate – live defense, coach will fungo from the plate. The base runners react to the depth and distance of the hit. The defense must finish the play focusing also on trail runner defense.

Round 10: Team Base Running – Situational

- Runner at 3rd and a hitter running at the plate – live defense, coach will fungo Texas Leaguers from home plate. The defense must finish the play.

Round 11: Bunt/Slap Defense – Situational

- Runner at 1st and a left handed slapper/bunter at home – live pitcher, catcher and defense *(pitcher is throwing fastballs only and the slapper is allowed to soft slap and bunt only)*.

Round 12: Live Scrimmage Using Situational Cards

- Two teams will be competing.
- The pitcher is a coach who normally pitches BP.

- The hitter and base runners from the offensive team will grab a card from a shuffled deck. Each card indicates where the base runner is located, what the count is and how many outs there are.
- Each team will bat through the entire line-up before switching to defense.
- Points are awarded based on the number of runs scored.
- The losing team will run a 60-yard sprint for every run scored by their opponent minus the number of runs that they scored (run differential).

Lisa (Sweeney) Van Ackeren

Princeton Practice Plan

Timed Warm-Up (15:00)

Throwing progression and everydays routine, with a time cap

Pregame Lines (8:00)

Regulated the way a pregame would be, limited reps, high energy

Team Defense (45:00)

Seven innings versus team rival

- Only nine players on the field at a time. Others are running the bases, rotating players in every two innings. Play it like a real game.
- Coaches regulate the number of runs the team scores on offense.
- Describe how we scored runs for visualization—Rachel led off with a soft slap single to short, Ashley moved her over with a great sac bunt on the first strike of the at-bat, and Krista drove Rachel in on a 3-2 count to the left-center gap.
- Key review questions:
  - What went well?
  - What can we work on?
  - How was our communication? Effort? What were our controllables?

Bat Warm-Up (5:00)

Focused on mental preparation to hit. Players should find their own space around the field to get loose quietly.

Hitting Circuit (8:00 Per Station, 45:00 Total With Switches)

Each player picks a partner who motivates her in hitting. Partners compete with each other for the rest of practice.

Circuit

1. Hoop tee: How many line drives go through the hoop hanging at the opposite end of the cage?
2. Directional front toss:
   - Must hit the ball where it's pitched. If she does not (i.e., pulls an outside pitch), she switches with her partner.
   - How many were successful?
3. Batting practice on field versus full circle pitch:
   - Ten reps, one sac bunt, one hit and run, one suicide squeeze
   - How many line drives, bunts, and hit and runs were executed successfully?

4. Shag at positions.
5. Pick your poison tee—the player chooses a drill we've worked on so far this year that helps her swing and addresses improvements that she is trying to make.

Total points, announce winner.

Pitching and Catching Workout (30:00)

- Four innings of batters (hitters tracking, rotate in for full at-bats)
- Point values:

  +1 for first-pitch strike

  +2 for killer off-speed pitch

  +3 for great strikeout pitch (movement and location)

  +4 for 1-2-3 inning

  −1 for pass ball or wild pitch
- Pitcher and catcher combo with the most points at the completion of four innings wins.

Dot Richardson, MD

Liberty University Practice Plan

2:00–2:30 p.m. Classroom

- Mental training exercises
- Video analysis session

2:30–3:00 p.m. Warm-Up

- Dynamic exercises
- Arm band stretches
- Defensive buddy concentration drills

  Purpose: to reinforce proper mechanics and to make them instinctive through repetition. Emphasize proper execution of these mechanics during the drills.

  Design:

  Teammates pair up.

  They set up about 12 feet (3.5 m) apart.

  Players roll ground balls slowly to each other, first directly at each other. They freeze after the ball contacts the glove and place the throwing hand on top.

  Next, they roll in a sideways direction of forehands to backhands for five of each and then work the way back.

  Each time, athletes focus on the fundamentals of having the glove out in front of the forehead and seeing the ball into the glove.

  Athletes freeze after fielding the ball into the glove. They focus purposefully on the ball and the feeling of fielding. Remember: quality, not quantity.

  Next, they execute pop-up tosses to each other.

  They continue to focus on receiving the ball with proper mechanics.

- Offensive buddy concentration drills

  Purpose: to reinforce proper mechanics and to make instinctive through repetition

  Design:

  Teammates pair up.

  One is the hitter with a bat.

  The other holds the ball for six pitch positions:

    High inside

    Waist high inside

    Low inside

    High outside

Waist high outside

Low outside

The hitter goes through the proper mechanics of the swing with each position.

Phase I and phase II

Always with a focus on the ball and the knob of the bat, the back foot, belly button, and nose should be pointing toward it in proper mechanics at the end of phase II.

Then the athletes switch roles.

Repeat this sequence of pitch selections, but this second time by advancing to phases I, II, and III, this time with proper mechanics with the mid-bat position and then to contact.

- Throwing progressions

  Partners start close and use proper mechanics.

  Advance distance between players based on defensive positions played.

3:00–3:30 p.m. Outfielders Position Defense, Infielders Hitting

- Outfielders take their defensive positions.

  Purpose: to have the outfielders receive balls hit to them from home plate simulating game-like directions, conditions, and situations

  Design: No throws; the goal of this drill is to have the fielders focus only on receiving the ball, not the throw.

  Two assistants hit balls from home plate.

  One hits to the left and center fielders.

  The other hits to right fielders.

  Direction of hit balls from home plate:

  Fly balls hit at the defenders

  Fly balls hit to the defenders' left

  Fly balls hit to the defenders' right

  Base hit ground balls hit at the defenders

  Ground balls hit to the defenders' left

  Ground balls hit to the defenders' right

  Repeat ground balls and sequence but this time simulate extra-base hit

  Repeat ground balls and sequence but this time simulate runner on second base situation

  Repeat ground balls and sequence, but this time simulate do-or-die situation with runner on second base

  Setup:

  Two empty buckets at each fielder position—left-field line, deep center, and right-field line

  Ball caddy or bucket at each hitter

  If possible, someone tossing balls to assistants hitting at home plate

- Infielders hit (batting cages or nearby area)

  Purpose: to focus on hitting mechanics and hitting weaknesses or scouting needs for upcoming competition

  Design: hitting stations (number of stations based on number of athletes)

  Tee work

  Bunting

  Phase I and phase II

  Soft toss

  Dry swing mechanic station

  Front toss

  Pitching machine

  Live pitching tracking

  Live pitching hitting

3:30–4:00 p.m. Infielders Crossfire Defense; Catchers, Pitchers, and Outfielders Hitting

- Infielders crossfire

  Purpose: to hit balls to infielders to reinforce proper fielding mechanics and simulate game situations

  Design:

  Two assistants hit balls from home plate.

  Sequence of hitting ground balls for assistant 1: 5-4, 4-5, 6-4, 4-6, 5-6, 6-5

  Sequence of hitting ground balls for assistant 2: 6-3, 3-6, 5-3, 3-5, 4-3, 3-4

  After the fielder receives the ball, she puts it in local bucket.

  Setup:

  Empty buckets at each base

  Ball caddie or buckets next to hitters at home plate

- Next, catchers

  Purpose: To focus on proper mechanics in pickoffs, throw-downs, and bunt defense

  Design:

  Front toss one pitch at a time to the catcher as she throws to first base, second base, and third base.

  From the batter's box, drop a bunt for the catcher to field and throw to the sequence of bases—first base, second base, and third base—using different infielders to cover the bases based on game situations.

  Call out different game situations after the first time through with different positions covering bases for each bunt.

- Then, pitchers

  Purpose: to focus on proper mechanics in fielding and throwing to bases

Design:

Hit balls to pitchers after they deliver their windup.

One pitcher at a time throws to first base, second base, third base, and home plate.

- Outfielder hitting (see infield hitting design and setup)

4:00–4:30 p.m. Infield and Outfield Situation Drills

Purpose: to simulate game situations requiring outfielders and infielders to communicate

Design:

All defenders take their positions on the field.

Coach hits balls from home plate to simulate all defensive situations that require infielders and outfielder to work together.

Base hits to outfielders with throws to each base (fly balls and ground balls)

Watch infielders' positioning:

Middle infielders for relay plays, short cutoffs, and throws to bases or home plate

Corners for cutoff positioning and throws to bases or home plate

Hits between outfielders

Hits between outfielders and infielders

Fair and foul hits

- Bunt coverage

With infielders, outfielders, pitchers, catchers

Include situations: Number of outs, batter's position in the lineup, location of batter at the plate, score of the game, inning

4:30–5:00 p.m. Specific Defensive Situations or Scrimmage

5:15–6:15 p.m. Strength and Conditioning

Ken Ericksen

South Florida Practice Plan

When warming up, warm up! When practicing your skills, work!				
0:00–0:10	Dynamics			
0:10–:20	Throwing program			
Caring starts from how competitive you are when you practice!				
0:20–0:50	Defensive skill work OF, IF, C			
0:50–1:15	Team defense 1: cutoffs and relays			
1:15–1:35	Team defense 2: first-and-third defense			
1:35–1:55	Team offense 1: baserunning from home to first			
1:55–2:15	Team defense 2: short game live with pitchers (one strike per batter)			
How long can you maintain focus?				
2:15–3:30	Hitting practice			
Live	Batting cage	Batting cage	Defense, live	Baserunning
Player 1	Player 4	Player 7	Player 10	Player 13
Player 2	Player 5	Player 8	Player 11	Player 14
Player 3	Player 6	Player 9	Player 12	Player 15
1. 2 bunts, 3 opposite 2. 3 hit aways 3. 3 hit aways, bunt for hit 4. hit and run, 3 hit aways 5. 3 hit aways, squeeze	Center toss	Tee work	Live at position	Baserunning at second base (trying to score)
0:10–0:20	30 feet (10 m) with step, side mechanics, 45 degrees, elbow position; love your glove			
2 min.	45 feet (15 m) footwork on receiving; reset; release points and finish			
3 min.	60 feet (20 m) progressive on intensity; release and finish			
2 min.	75 feet (25 m) getting off the back side			

Celeste Knierim

St. Louis Community College of Meramec Practice Plan

Preseason Practice in the Gym

(Details of some drills may be found in Chapter 8)

Warm-Ups

- Agility workout – various drills done with ladder, cones, spots, lines on floor
- In and outs – like suicides but with a ball and gloves involving catch and throw
- Football – coach throws, players run specific patterns, receive ball and throw to specific areas
- Finish throwing warm ups

Drills

1A on half of gym with outfielders/pitchers

- Quick four person bunting for a hit drill off of machine without defense
- Quick four person slapping drill without defense
- Bunting/slapping drills with the defense

1B on other half of gym with infielders/catchers

- ground ball drills with line drives
- throwing on the run
- over the head
- bunts
- short hops
- back hand
- up the middle
- in the gaps
- foul ball pop-ups/line drives

2A infielders and catchers do slap and bunt drills

2B (Low ceiling so fly ball drills have to be outside)

- outfielders and pitchers do line drives
- bloops
- two-person tweeners
- foul balls

- grounders and relays
- Practice with pressure/working on situational plays

1A Infielders work on grounders.

- Outfielders, extra pitchers and catchers are runners.
- Runners are told to be very aggressive but smart.
- Puts pressure on the fielders and gives them a better idea of how quick they need to be to get the out and how they need to think ahead and be ready for the second and third play.

1B Outfielders work on line drives, bloops, down the line, off the fence (wall), tweeners, etc.

- Infielders, extra catchers and pitchers are running.
- Can start runners on any base and home to work on certain situations.

Finish practice with a short game with pitcher, put runners on bases for situations, work on steals, delay steals, squeezes, breaking off bases to put pressure on defense and pitcher/catcher.

Connie Clark

Texas Practice Plan

Team Warm-Up (25 Minutes)

Dynamic stretching, sprints, band work, throw, focus catch, and dailies

Defense Rotation 1 (14 Minutes)

- Coach and two managers work three stations doing rolled ground balls for 7 minutes and hand-tossed fly balls for 7 minutes. Outfielders work fundamentals of receiving and making throws into sock nets. Athletes rotate lines to coach (three nets and three buckets of balls).
- MG, LS, RS, SW, HK, TM, MK, AA, KH
- KS and CC hit ground ball reps for 7 minutes. CC hit ground balls to pitchers and they alternate on making play to first and second. When play made to second middle infielder, finish out double play. SC/DT trade coverage and KS receives at first for 7 minutes (balls, bats, protective net at second).
- DT, SC, EW, LS, GS, T, KC
- Coach and manager work with catchers: footwork and transitions on steal throws to second and picks to first. Time and record (balls, plate, and set up first and second base distances, protective net).
- ES, RL, TK

Defense Rotation 2 (14 Minutes)

- Coach—middle infield work and drills, KS—first-base work and drills (14 minutes) (balls, other equipment)
- SC, DT, KH, AA, HK, TM, MK
- Coach and manager—third-base pen to begin pitching workout (14 minutes plus 12 minutes of first offense round and then join offense for final two rounds).
- GS, TD, KC, RL, ES, manager/EW begins with spin work and walk through into a zone in on left-field foul area (plate, protective net behind zone in).
- Coach and manager—work outfield drills and challenges with throws to plate from left field, work with infield group for last 5 minutes) (balls, protective nets, other equipment)
- MG, LS, RS, SW, TK

Offense (40 Minutes Total, Three Stations, 12 Minutes Each)

- Two offense groups (cage or field) with the same three stations set up in each area
  - RHs: HK, TM, KC/MK, KH, ES/RS, RL, TK
  - LHs: DT, LS, GS/MG, AA, TD/SC, SW

- Pitchers and catchers miss first hitting station to finish pitching workout. Keep groups intact for balance.
- Station 1 (drills, individual work, film and watch Dartfish Express)
- Station 2 (tossing, location focus)
- Station 3 (live with specific focus)

Challenge of the Day (10 Minutes)

Split team in half. Have them compete against each other with specific drills or put an athlete on the spot to have one shot to complete a task.

Bill Gray and Melissa Chmielewski

Missouri Southern Practice Plan

Throwing program		Emphasis
One-knee flips	1–2 minutes	Ball rotation
One-knee technique	1–2 minutes	Release point and follow-through
Four-count throwing	5–10 minutes	Open up, elbows up, throw, and follow-through
Long toss	3–5 minutes	Use legs, lift weights for the throw
Position throws	3–5 minutes	Focus and execution
Team throwing drill	3–5 minutes	Accuracy and release
Position work—skills that need to be reviewed on the day		**Team defense—skills that need to be reviewed for the weekend or upcoming game**
Middles		Outfield throw to bases
Corners		Infield crossfire
Catchers		Next-play throwing
Outfielders		Slap defense
		21 out scouting report

Lonni Alameda

Florida State Practice Plan

Early Work

Each Hitting Group Works for 1 Hour

Start in Cages (Don't waste reps on a live arm, make sure to warm up.)

- Tee work, center toss, and bunts (machine set in bullpen)

Batting Practice on Field (half running, half hitting)

- 1st round: Situational hitting (2 bunts, 2 hit and run, 2 get 'em over, 2 get 'em in)
- 2nd round: 7 swings - running at second base reads
- 3rd round: 3 swings - running at third reads
- Runners and hitters switch

Defensive Reps (Will mix into batting practice on Thursday.)

- Infield ground ball reps
- Outfield do or die and balls off the wall
- Catchers reps off machine in bullpen and plays at the plate

Jo Evans

Texas A&M Practice Plan

3:15–3:35 Jog, stretch, team sprints (on own)

3:35–3:40 Coach talks practice plan with the team.

Splits—outfield in the cages, infield on defense

Warm up arms

3:50–4:20 Infield on defense, outfield in cages

Infield defense:
- Two-batter infield
- Plays at home

4:20–4:50 Outfield on defense, infield in cages

Outfield defense:
- Outfield in positions—hit routine balls to warm up
- Balls overhead, hold-your-ground balls, balls in front
- Throw home—two fly balls and two grounders

Cage work: station work, tees, machines, front toss, BP

4:55 Water break

5:00–5:30 Team defense

Cutoffs and relays

21 Outs

5:30–6:30 Live hitting off pitchers with defense

6:30–6:45 Jog, stretch, huddle up, and evaluate practice.

Do an Aggie Yell!

Donna Papa

Carolina Practice Plan

2:15   Weights @ Wt Room

3:15   Team Meeting

3:45   Practice

Warm Ups: Throw/Dailies (NO dynamics –done in wt room)

3:55   Defense: IF/OF – Split& Pitchers – Syd & Fuller – Bullpen

IF- Rhythm Drill

IF - Crossfire Drill w/ Baseballs- *1 min each fielder*- small gloves – 4 hitters- 15 min- DJP/CB/MJ/

& OF – Tennis balls- no gloves – one hand – Kayla -15 min

Balls in front – 5 min

Balls over shoulder – 5 min

Balls at Fence – 5 min

4:10   Queen of Diamond Challenge – 2 Defenses- Goal is to stay on field/ Make error – come off field- 7 min each defense

D#1:   LF/TW/KB/DR/DG/AM/EW/KL/KB

D#2:   LM/ES/EC/KS/BD/DD/KS/TC/SM/JF

4:20   Bunt D Challenge – 3 Teams/ 12 min per group

Goal:

Have the most # of BR advance ; > # of bases - WINNER – Push /Sac/Quick Slap

12 min – ½ team bunts/ other half BR

If you let strike go by – immed run to RF fence

If you pop up pitch – immed run to RF fence

Attempt – let ball go by – immed run to fence

PITCHERS: Rotate 3 hitters ea/ switch – Syd and Fuller

5:00   Water Break

Offensive Stations:

#1   Two Lane Front Toss – on field: MJ/DJP

Low pitches – 2 sides: 1.Inside & 2. Outside

#2   Shag Group – Work on getting to balls- Bucket

#3   In Cage – Machine- Set speed – 65 mph – Mgr feed (radar gun)

Rounds:

a. Tar Heel – 4 cuts

b. Swing- 4

#4   Live in Cage-CB Fast /Slow

Jen McIntyre

UCONN Practice Plan

This practice is my favorite because the team is able to see all the pieces of the puzzle come together. After a team focuses for a couple of weeks on the breakdown of specific defensive sets, set plays, and offensive situations, this practice can give the feel of live game situations and build confidence going into a tough weekend series.

Objectives

1. To review several game situations and have the team execute each one properly
2. To have players compete with each other and to challenge the team to raise each standard
3. To have the team see success and be fast and efficient throughout the innings

How It Works

The team runs, stretches, and throws (RST) as they normally do and then performs an infield and outfield breakdown of everyday drills to get warmed up. After they are warm, the seven innings begin. Each "inning" is made up of a specific defensive play or situation that the team must complete successfully before they move on to the next inning. After each inning the team must hustle off and on the field as they would in a game. At UCONN, we define hustle as simply "faster than they're moving now." By nature, this turns into a sprint. I challenge the farthest outfielder to sprint off and on from the dugout to her position in six seconds or less (always attention to detail). If the team does not perform the sprint in that time, we do it again.

The seven innings can consist of whatever sets you want to focus on as you move into each weekend series. Regardless of the opponent, I always like to include bunt defense and situations. As you create the innings, you set standards in which they must complete each task successfully to move on. For example, in an inning of first-and-third defense I may tell them we need eight outs to get out of the inning. An inning may focus on outfield throwing to bases. The outfielders are all out at their positions and must make three perfect throws to each base before we are done with the inning. (For this one, have your infielders kneeling to receive at the bases so that the throws have to be pinpoint accurate). For an inning of bunt defense, we may need 10 total outs, with at least 5 occurring at second base. To add some fun, double the points to challenge them to keep going for the lead out. You can obviously adjust numbers to suit your specific personnel, but keep in mind that this practice is designed for success and confidence. You can either put your starting defense out there all the time or mix in potential subs each inning. For example, in the situational defense inning I establish three rotations and tell the team we need 12 outs from each rotation before the inning is over. Note that sprinting must occur after each rotational change.

Have fun with it and keep it fast paced. As a reward for completing the seven innings, we always finish with Dr. Feel Good double front toss on the field.

Husky 7-Inning Practice

Inning	Task	Scoring
1	Bunt defense (runner at first)	10 outs, at least 5 at second
2	First-and-third defense	10 points needed (2 for an out with no run scored, 3 for two outs on the same play, 1 point if runners are forced back to original base, –1 if runner advances to second, –3 if the run scores)
3	Outfield throw to bases	Three perfect throws to each base
4	Defensive situations	12 outs by three rotations
5	Wild pitches and passed balls	8 outs at the plate
6	RBI hitting (runners at second and third)	15 runs scored (all with less than two outs to incorporate hitting behind the runner and sac flies, reset every time; we use a BP pitcher for this)
7	Steal throws (runner at first, runner at second)	Each catcher needs 5 outs at each base
Extra innings	Dr. Feel Good (easy BP) double front toss	No scoring needed, easy batting practice

Other options for innings:

- Pitchers throwing to bases
- Continuous rundowns

  Continuous rundowns begin by placing a runner between first and second. As soon as the out is made there, a secondary on-deck runner jumps in between third and home. The defender who made the original out charges across the field to begin the rundown between third and home. After that out is made, another runner jumps in again between first and second. This sequence goes on for three rotations, or six outs. We reset after six outs to allow defensive changes. If we do this drill in the seven-inning practice, we can complete three or four defensive rotations. This competitive drill encourages the defense to get out of their robotic comfort zone and fill in wherever they are needed. Often, they end up covering bases they don't naturally cover, but they need to become accustomed to doing so when broken plays happen in a game.

- Squeeze offense or defense
- Baserunning reads from second base
- Thread the needle (balls between 3B, SS,CF, and LF and between RF, CF, 2B, and 1B)
- Relays to home, mix in cuts called to back bases

About the NFCA

The National Fastpitch Coaches Association (NFCA) is the professional growth organization for fastpitch softball coaches from all competitive levels of play.

The idea for a softball coaching association first developed from discussions at the National Collegiate Women's Softball Championships in the early 1980s. Although mostly collegiate coaches constituted the organization's membership in the early days, today's collegiate coaches are joined by high school and club coaches and umpires as well as other fans of fastpitch softball.

Besides services offered to the membership, the NFCA works with USA Today to produce polls for NCAA Division I and high school softball. NCAA Division II and Division III polls are also produced. In addition, the NFCA conducts collegiate tournament competitions and recruiting camps around the country.

Dr. JoAnne Graf retired after serving as Head Softball Coach at Florida State University for 30 years. She ended her coaching career leading all coaches in the country with 1,437 total wins. Her final record was 1437-478-6. Her tenure included winning two Association of Intercollegiate Athletics for Women (AIAW) National Slow Pitch Softball Championships, 10 Atlantic Coast Conference (ACC) Softball Championships and 7 National Collegiate Athletic Association Softball World Series appearances. Six times she has been named as the ACC Coach of the Year and four times as the National Fast Pitch Coaches Association (NFCA) Region Coach of the Year. Graf was inducted into the NFCA Hall of Fame in 2003. In 2013, Dr. Graf was inducted into the Florida State University Athletics Hall of Fame. Graf has contributed to the growth of Fast Pitch Softball by serving on the Executive Board of the NFCA as a member of the Ethics Committee and as the Emeriti Chair. She has also served on the NCAA Softball Committee, All American and All Region Committees.

Her teams had 21 NCAA Tournament appearances with 45 NCAA tournament victories. Player accolades include 35 All Americans, 84 ACC Honor Roll selections, 74 All ACC selections, and 96 All Region awards. Six players were named as ACC Player of the Year, 6 were named as ACC Rookie of the Year and 10 ACC Tournament MVP's. Graf has also coached two Honda Broderick Award Winners (Darby Cottle and Jessica van der Linden), and in 2004, Jessica van der Linden was named as the USA National Softball Player of the Year.

After retiring from coaching, Dr. Graf joined the Sport Management Faculty at Florida State. She is a renowned clinician and speaker who has spoken at softball clinics all over the country. Her writings have included a book *Championship Slow Pitch Softball*, a chapter on ethics in *She Can Coach* and a chapter on organizing a winning softball program in *The Softball Coaching Bible*. She has taught classes in Introduction to Sport Management, Principles and Problems of Coaching, Diversity in Sport, Governance in Sport, Human Resources, Issues in Sport Management, Personnel Administration, Softball Techniques, Theory and Practice of Softball. Other duties included supervising the Lifetime Activities Program and serving as the Teaching Assistant Liaison for the Department of Sport Management at FSU.

About the Contributors

Lonni Alameda has been the head coach at Florida State since 2009. The Seminoles have earned four ACC regular-season championships, won three ACC tournament championships, and made six appearances in the ACC championship game. In the NCAA tournament, FSU has reached the NCAA super regional round in each of the last three seasons and appeared in the Women's College World Series in 2014. Alameda came to Florida State after five seasons at UNLV and has a career record of 472-278-1 (.629), a 315-120 (.724) mark at Florida State, and a 116-37 (.758) record in ACC play. She has coached 23 NFCA All-Americans during her career, including 2014  USA Softball National Player of the Year Lacey Waldrop. Alameda has been named ACC Coach of the Year in each of the last three seasons (2013–15), won MWC Coach of the Year honors at UNLV in 2005 and 2007, and was chosen as the 2005 NFCA West Region Coach of the Year.

 **Melissa Chmielewski** begins her fifth year of coaching softball. After one year as the assistant she takes over the helm at Missouri Southern State University. Chmielewski played her collegiate career at NCAA Division I North Dakota State University where she played first base from 2007 to 2010. Melissa was a two-time Summit League Player of the Year (2010 and 2008), a 2010 CoSIDA College Division first-team Academic All-American, a 2010 Summit League All-Tournament team selection, a 2010 and 2009 Louisville Slugger–NFCA All-Midwest Region first-team selection, a three time All-Summit League first-team selection, a 2008 Louisville Slugger–NFCA All-Midwest Region second-team selection, a three-time NFCA Scholar Athlete, a 2009 *ESPN the Magazine* Academic All-District first-team selection, a two-time Summit League Winter–Spring All-Academic selection, a two-time Summit League Commissioner's List of Academic Excellence selection, a 2007 Division I Independent Newcomer of the Year, and a 2007 All-Independent first-team selection.

Helping the Bison transition from Division II to Division I, Chmielewski, was a part of the four-year period that saw NDSU go 142-85 overall and 47-14 in their first three years in the Summit League. Winning Summit League titles in

2009 and 2010, Melissa and the Bison made two NCAA regional appearances. In 2009 NDSU knocked off perennial power Oklahoma in the opening game of the Norman regional and advanced to the Tempe, Arizona, super regional before falling to the defending WCWS champions, Arizona State, two games to none. In 2010 the Bison put up a 33-25 overall record, including a 14-8 Summit League mark, and advanced to the Seattle regional.

Connie Clark became the head coach of the University of Texas softball program in 1996 and has since built one of the most successful programs in college softball. In 19 varsity seasons, Clark has given Texas softball its reputation for having the best players, facilities, traditions, and coaches. When people talk about Texas softball, they talk about only one thing: success.

Since its ascension to varsity status in 1997, Texas, under Clark's direction, has emerged as one of the most dominant softball programs in the nation. In 19 seasons at the helm of the varsity program, Clark—the 1987 Broderick National Softball Player of the Year as a collegian—has led UT to five Women's College World Series appearances (1998, 2003, 2005, 2006, 2013), 16 NCAA tournament appearances (1998–2000, 2002–03, 2005–15), four Big 12 Conference tournament titles (1999, 2002, 2003, 2005), and four Big 12 regular-season titles (2002, 2003, 2006, 2010). In fact, Texas' appearance in the 1998 WCWS, in just its second varsity season, still ranks as the quickest arrival at the NCAA Division I softball "elite eight" tournament in the history of the sport.

Clark has amassed 769 overall wins, for an average of more than 40 victories a season, and produced one national player of the year (three times), 28 All-America selections, 65 all-region selections, 93 All-Big 12 Conference choices, and six academic All-Americans.

The head coach of the USF softball team since 1997, boasting an 819-424-1 career record, **Ken Eriksen** has ended the season with a winning record on 17 occasions. While at the helm of one of the most successful programs on campus, Eriksen has led 11 teams to the NCAA Regional, won Regional Championships in 2006 and 2012, and won the 2012 Super Regional to advance to the school's first ever Women's College World Series. Eriksen has also won four conference titles, including a BIG EAST Regular Season title in 2008 and the program's first BIG EAST Tournament Championship in 2013. Eriksen has also been the head coach of the women's national team since 2011 and led the Red, White and Blue to four World Cup of Softball titles. Eriksen lives in Tampa with his wife Debra and his two daughters, Tatiana and Natasha.

Jo Evans has been the head coach at Texas A&M University since the summer of 1996. During her tenure, the Aggies have reached new heights, appearing in 16 NCAA regionals, five NCAA super regionals, and two NCAA Women's College World Series. During the 2014 season, Evans became the only active Southeastern Conference head coach to eclipse the 1,000 career win mark and earned her 700th win in Aggieland. With a stellar career record of 1062-574-2 (.649), Evans was inducted into the NFCA Hall of Fame in December 2015.

Bill Gray coached the game of softball for 25 years and had experience at almost every level. He was a student assistant at Pittsburg State University (NCAA Division II) from 1991 to 1993. He spent one year at his alma mater, Pittsburg High School, before starting the program at Independence Community College in Independence, Kansas. He returned to NCAA Division II coaching for six years at Francis Marion University in Florence, South Carolina. He then moved on to Kennesaw State University in Georgia as the program transitioned from Division II to Division I. He completed his softball career at Missouri Southern State University in Joplin, Missouri. He spent most of his career putting programs back on the map. In his one year at PHS he won three times as many games in one year as they had in the first two. At Francis Marion he took a nonexistent program and moved it into a regional contender. Kennesaw State was an established program that competed in 13 national tournaments in its 15 years at Division II. In 2005 KSU finished second in the country in its last year of Division II competition. Most recently, Gray served as the head coach of Missouri Southern. Gray was an active member of the National Fastpitch Coaches Association. He served on several committees, was the Division II representative on the national board for 10 years, and was the driving force behind the NFCA Division II National Player of the Year and Freshman of the Year awards that were first given in 2015.

Rachel Hanson begins her second year as Stanford's head coach in 2015–16. She guided the Cardinal to wins against five NCAA tournament teams and single-season numbers in multiple offensive categories that ranked among the top 10 in program history.

Hanson took the reins at Stanford after four seasons as the Dartmouth head coach, where she elevated the program to new levels of success and claimed the winningest seasons in the school's past decade.

Hanson had a successful 2014 season in which she led the Big Green to its first Ivy League championship with an 18-2 conference record (31-19 overall) and a trip to the NCAA Tempe regional. Before leading the Big Green, Hanson coached the University of Dallas softball team for five seasons and set a program record of 80 wins.

A 2005 graduate of Trinity with a degree in political science, Hanson was a three-time all-conference selection and captained her team to a conference championship in her senior year. She was a force in the classroom as well, earning academic all-conference honors and receiving recognition on the Dean's List.

Celeste Knierim, who was inducted into the NFCA Hall of Fame in 2003 after 30 years in coaching, made her name at St. Louis Community College at Meramec. She joined the staff there in 1973 and didn't leave until her retirement in 2004. She also served as an associate professor of physical education and coach for volleyball, basketball, and field hockey at some time during her tenure. Knierim's heralded softball coaching career culminated with 1,043 victories (1,043-542), making her the all-time winningest coach in the history of NJCAA softball, a record that stood for seven years after her retirement. She earned a spot in *Sports Illustrated*'s "Faces in the Crowd" for claiming her 1,000th career victory in 2004.

During her storied career, she led the Magic to 16 appearances in the NJCAA national championship and garnered 25 conference titles. At nationals, Knierim's teams placed in the top five 11 of 16 years, including three second-place finishes.

For her success, she earned numerous regional and conference coaching accolades, and many of her players were recognized. Forty-five were named NJCAA All-American, and 39 were NFCA All-American. She had 125 all-conference and 119 all-region selections as well.

Also involved in coaching at the international level, Knierim was in the USA coaching pool from 2000 to 2008, as well as coach and later administrator for NJCAA All-Star teams participating in Canada Cup from 1993 through 2002. She was involved in the NJCAA, serving as president of the NJCAA Softball Coaches Association from 1994 to 1996 as well as vice-president and secretary before being elected president. Knierim has been recognized by numerous halls of fame in addition to the NFCA, including the NJCAA (1999), St. Louis/Meramec Athletics (2002), St. Louis ASA (2004), and NJCAA Region 16 (2007). She was the winner of the St. Louis Women of Achievement Award in 2000 and the Sigma Kappa Sorority Colby Award in 2006.

Also a noted clinician, Knierim continues to teach softball, conduct clinics, coach teams on tours internationally, and administer tournaments in the St. Louis area.

Entering her ninth season as UK's head coach, **Rachel Lawson** is beginning to realize her vision for the Kentucky softball program. The winningest head coach in program history has led UK to its first-ever appearance in the Women's College World Series, reached the NCAA super regionals three times in the last four seasons, and achieved a program-best 50 wins in 2014. UK's administration come through on their promise and commitment to softball by providing Lawson with one of the nation's best collegiate softball facilities in the $9.5 million John Cropp Stadium. Lawson and company have made sure that the beautiful stadium has seen lots of wins over the past few seasons as UK had its two most successful seasons in program history.

In 2014 Lawson guided Kentucky to the Women's College World Series. The Wildcats also set single-season records in at-bats, runs scored, doubles, home runs, RBIs, total bases, walks, fielding percentage, putouts, lowest ERA, and strikeouts. UK, which advanced to the program's first SEC tournament championship, started the season with a program-best 12 straight wins.

Julie Lenhart begins her 22nd season as head softball coach at SUNY Cortland in 2016. She is the program's all-time wins leader with a record of 701-268-2, and her overall record of 821-345-2 (including five seasons at Wisconsin–Platteville) makes her one of only eight coaches in Division III history to reach the 800-win mark.

Lenhart's Cortland teams have qualified for the NCAA Division III playoffs 14 times, most recently in 2015. Her squads have made seven World Series appearances, including a national runner-up showing in 2013 and a fourth-place finish in 2011. Lenhart was inducted into the National Fastpitch Coaches Association (NFCA) Hall of Fame in December 2014.

Jen McIntyre is in her second season as the head coach at the University of Connecticut. Before arriving in Storrs, McIntyre served as the associate head coach at Boston University for the 2014 season. The Terriers won the Patriot League tournament and qualified for the NCAA regionals. McIntyre joined the Terriers after spending 12 years (2002–13) on the Penn State coaching staff, including the last three as associate head coach. During her tenure, PSU reached six NCAA tournaments, highlighted by a regional final appearance in 2011. Twenty-one of McIntyre's recruits at PSU were named to All-Big Ten teams 33

times, seven were placed on the all-region squads, and three became NFCA All-Americans. She spent the 2000 and 2001 seasons at Indiana as the second assistant coach.

Donna Papa, the NFCA Hall of Fame head softball coach at North Carolina since 1986, has helped build Carolina softball into one of the top programs in the country. Papa has led Carolina to the NCAA tournament in 12 of the last 15 years, five regular-season ACC titles, and the 2001 ACC tournament crown. During the 2011 season, the five-time ACC Coach of the Year became the 11th Division I head coach to win 1,000 career games, and Papa currently ranks sixth among active Division I head coaches in career victories (1,155-632-5). She has helped nine players earn 12 NFCA All-America honors and 63 players attain All-Southeast Region honors. In addition to achieving success on the field, Papa's program is known for excellence in the classroom. Christine Kubin earned academic All-America honors in 1995 and 1996, and 11 other Tar Heels have earned a total of 16 academic all-district selections.

Before arriving in Chapel Hill, Papa spent two seasons as head volleyball and softball coach at Susquehanna University. She served as an assistant softball coach at St. John's University from 1981 to 83 after spending one year as an assistant coach at UNC Greensboro while in graduate school. Papa earned a bachelor's degree in physical education from the University of Connecticut in 1979. She played four seasons of softball for the Huskies and was cocaptain during her junior and senior seasons. Papa's playing career also encompassed stints with ASA Major Fastpitch teams including the Franklin Coronets (West Haven, Connecticut) and the Waterford (Connecticut) Mariners.

Dot Richardson, MD is the head softball coach at Liberty University in Lynchburg, Virginia. She is also a motivational speaker, author, surgeon, and world-class athlete. Athletically, through the sport of fast-pitch softball, Dot has received numerous accolades, highlighted by becoming a two-time Olympic gold medalist (softball 1996 and 2000), NCAA Player of the Decade (1980s), five-time world champion, and five-time Pan American champion. She has participated in many other international competitions representing the United States all over the world. Dot made her first USA team at the age of 17 and her last at the 2000 Olympic Games in Sydney, Australia. She is a

5-time collegiate All-American and a 16-time Amateur Softball Association All-American. She was inducted into the UCLA Hall of Fame, the ASA Hall of Fame, and the State of Florida Hall of Fame.

Dot attended the University of California at Los Angeles (UCLA) and obtained her bachelor's degree in kinesiology, premed, while participating in softball and basketball. In softball she was named MVP each year. She was selected All-University Athlete of the Year during her senior year, sharing the honor with Olympic great Jackie Joyner. She received her master's degree in heath at Adelphi University in Garden City, Long Island, New York. She earned a medical degree from the University of Louisville, completed her orthopedic surgery residency program at the University of Southern California, and received fellowship training in orthopedic sports medicine from the world renowned Kerlan and Jobe Orthopedic Clinic in Los Angeles, where she worked with the Dodgers, Lakers, Sparks, Mighty Ducks, Avengers, Kings, and Galaxy.

Dot served under President George W. Bush for two terms as vice chair for the President's Council on Physical Fitness and Sports. She also served the State of Florida under Governor Charlie Crist on the Governor's Council on Physical Fitness.

Dot was born in Orlando, Florida. She traveled all over the United States and the world during her childhood because her father, Kenneth Richardson, served in the United States Air Force. He retired after 22 years of service as a senior master sergeant and settled his family in Union Park, Florida, just east of Orlando. In 2001 Dot married Bob Pinto and started her practice as an orthopedic surgeon. She was then hired by South Lake Hospital to be the director and medical director for the National Training Center. In 2013 Dot was hired as the head softball coach by Liberty University, the largest Christian university in the world, in Lynchburg, Virginia.

South Carolina has seen its star rise again in the collegiate softball world under the guidance of head coach **Beverly Smith**, who arrived in July of 2010. As a head coach, Smith's overall record is 157-131. She is only the second Gamecocks softball coach with more than 100 career wins.

The Gamecocks improved their record for the third consecutive season in 2015, the only SEC program that can stake that claim, and appeared in the NCAA tournament for the third time under Smith. Smith's squad also produced its first NFCA All-American, as left fielder Alaynie Page garnered a first-team spot. Before coming to South Carolina, Smith served as the top assistant at North Carolina. She was the lead recruiter for the Tar Heels during that time, helping to bring five All-Americans into the UNC program. She coached a pitching staff that ranked in the top 10 in the nation in ERA in three of her final four seasons at North Carolina.

A standout player for head coach Donna Papa before joining her staff, Smith was the 1994 ACC Player of the Year. Smith was honored as one of the top 50 softball players in ACC history during the league's 50th anniversary celebration in 2002. She played and served as an assistant coach for the Tampa Bay FireStix of the Women's Pro Softball League in 1997.

Lisa (Sweeney) Van Ackeren, a four-time Patriot League Pitcher of the Year at Lehigh and a New Jersey native, is in her fourth season as Princeton's head softball coach in 2016. In her first season Van Ackeren became the winningest first-year coach in Princeton softball history, finishing at 27-19, the team's best record since the Tigers went 34-19 in 2006. Princeton's 12-8 Ivy League record in Van Ackeren's first year was the program's best since 2008, when the team went 18-2.

Through three seasons Van Ackeren has a record of 62-69. She is already the fourth-winningest coach in program history. A 2009 Lehigh graduate, Van Ackeren coached as a volunteer assistant at Lehigh in 2010 and was an assistant coach at Penn in 2011 and 2012. When she finished her playing career at Lehigh, the former Lisa Sweeney's name was listed more than 100 times in the Patriot League record book. She is the only player ever to win four Patriot League Pitcher of the Year awards. She was the 2008 Patriot League Player of the Year and a third-team CoSIDA Academic All-America honoree in 2008. No one in Patriot League history had won more games (104), pitched more shutouts (31), pitched in more games (141), started more games (112), or finished more games (91). She completed her career with the Patriot League record for strikeouts in a career (928), as well as the top three single-season totals.

Three of her four seasons represented the top three single-season win totals in Patriot League history, and she also twice led the league in saves in a season. Her four no-hitters, including games thrown against Harvard and Penn, both in 2007, were a Patriot League record. Among those is a perfect game, thrown against Army as a freshman in the 2006 Patriot League tournament. Van Ackeren had a record of 94-28 as a pitcher at Lehigh, and the Mountain Hawks won 155 games over her four seasons. She pitched in three NCAA regionals, and Lehigh won at least one game in each, twice winning two.

In the 2012 season, her second as an assistant coach at Penn, Van Ackeren worked with unanimous first-team All-Ivy League selection Alexis Borden as the Quakers won the Ivy South division. Since coming to Princeton, Van Ackeren's players have earned eight All-Ivy League honors over her two seasons.